MW01181751

CHINA'S MINORITY PEOPLES

Edited by the State Nationalities Affairs Commission
Published by the China Pictorial Publishing House

The First Edition in August 1995;
The Second Edition in July 1996.

Consultants: Wen Jing, Tudao Duoji,
Li Jianyou, Zhang Jiahua
General planning: Wang Fulin, Yang Houdi,
Fa Hexi, Yang Fan
Directors: Yang Fan, Huang Zu'an
Deputy directors: Chen Leqi, Bao Shulin
Members: Li Chunsheng, Chen Yong,
Wang Qingshuo, Yang Liu,
Chen Yueping, Zhao Chunlin
Chief Editors: Li Chunsheng, Chen Yong
Designer: Shi Weiping
Translator: Jiang Ying
Edited by the State Commission of Nationality Affarirs
Published by China Pictorial Publishing House
Produced by Beijing Dongfang Mingzhu Cultural Development Co., Ltd.
8 The Forth Street, Shangdi, Haidian District,
Beijing, 100085, China.
Phone for Order: 62983406 - 32

Distributed by China International Book Trading Corporation
35 Chegongzhuang Xilu, Beijing
100044, China.
P.O. Box 399, Beijing, China.
ISBN7 - 80024 - 046 - 0/J - 047

Printed in the People's Republic of China.

INDEX

INTRODUCTION

In addition to the Han majority, China, with a land mass of 9.6 million square kilometers, is home to 55 minority ethnic groups, whose population totals 91 million. Though they make up only 8% of the national population, they are scattered across an extremely large area, covering about 64% of China's territory.

The splendid, more than 5,000-year long Chinese civilization, has had a profound influence on the development of Asian culture, and the world's. Meanwhile, the cultural heritage of Chinese ethnic groups make up an indispensable component of Chinese civilization.

Since ancient times, the minority groups and the Hans have amalgamated and gotten along with each other. Communal effort has made China a strong country with a vast land mass. In the course of its development, ethnic artists and scientists created a wealth of beautiful poems, myths, legends, music, dances, paintings and scientific works for their people and constructed many magnificent buildings. This picture album will give a brief introduction to the colorful ethnic customs including festivals, attire, marriage ceremonies and other rites.

In general, most Chinese ethnic groups make their homes in close-knit communities in the vast plateau, grassland and forest areas. On their beautiful land, they created and developed their civilizations.

Language is a product of culture as well as a bridge of communication. Among the 55 Chinese minority groups, 53 have their own languages, which belong to the many language branches of the Sino-Tibetan, Altaic, Indo-European, Austro-Asiatic and Austronesian language families. Twenty-one ethnic groups still use their own written systems. The primitive *Dongba* hieroglyphs of Naxi Nationality for example have been used for more than 1,000 years. Today, the *Dongba Classic* containing more than 1,500 kinds, over 20,000 volumes and involving philosophy, history, religion, medicine, astronomy, folk customs, literature and the arts are separately stored in the libraries and museums of Lijiang, Kunming, Nanjing, Beijing, Taiwan, America, Germany and France. They form an encyclopedia of the ancient Naxi society. Another hieroglyph is *Shuishu* used by the Shui Nationality. Though not many *Shuishu* books are left, they are valuable for research. The Yis use a syllabic written form, while the Mongolian, Tibetan, Uygur, Kazak and Dai languages use alphabetic system. The Dai language alone has four different written forms.

Owing to great regional and environmental diversity, different minority groups developed distinct life styles of their own. China has long been an agricultural society. Like the Hans, farming made up a vital part of the traditional economy among most ethnic groups. Some roamed on pasture land raising animals and a few hunted and fished. Today, as the market economy flourishes more and more in China each year, modern ways of life have become popular in many ethnic areas.

Most Chinese ethnic groups have their own religious beliefs. The major religions include Buddhist Lamaism, Hinayana, Islam, Christianity, Taoism, Shamanism, and primitive animism, totemism and polytheism. The spreading and development of these religious faiths brought forth a wealth of literary and artistic works such as the Tibetan's *Mahabharate, Sakya Bhanchihdha*, the Uygurs' *Kudaku Blik*, the Dais' *Sadujialuo*, the Manchu's *Shaman Nishan*, and *the Imperial Manchu's Sacrificial Rites*, and Yao's *Bienh Huangh Dage*.

As for ethnic attire, food, housing, festivals, wedding ceremonies and funerals, different peoples have their own values, but they influence each other. Attire is a good example for illustration. The costumes of different ethnic groups vary greatly from place to place and contend in bizarrerie and beauty, such as the Manchu *qipao*, the Tibetan *chuba*, the Mongolian robe and boots, the Uygur *qapan* and embroidered cap, the Yi Ca'erwa and hero knot, the Miao women's silver headdresses, the Dai straight skirt and the Naxi silver plates. They not only display the aesthetic tastes of different peoples, but also reflect the cultural heritage inherited from their ancestors. Today, these colorful ethnic costumes are highly regarded around the world.

Ethnic cuisine, mostly tending to fresh, sour and hot, came into being in accordance with the local environment, climate and produce. On the endless grasslands, the Mongolians and Kazaks prefer tea with milk, sour horse milk, and braised mutton; on the snow-capped plateau, Tibetans have *tsampa* and butter tea as their staple diet; by rivers, the Hezhens consume fresh fish; in the Changbai mountains, Koreans prepare unique pickled vegetables and *dagao*; in warm and humid Xishuangbanna, the Dais are fond of *duosheng*, roast fish, and rice cooked in bamboo tubes. Their meals of flowers and insects are unique. In addition, an endless array of ethnic food such as Uygur *nang*, mutton rice, and kabobs, Bai rice pilaf and chicken, Yi *Tuotuo* meat, Naxi loquat meat, Miao fish slices in sour soup and beer duck, Dong sour fish, oil tea and block-the-way wine are thoroughly enjoyable and unforgettable.

Nearly every ethnic group developed a unique way of building suitable to local conditions with their wisdom and accumulation of life experience, and each has its advantages. The Hezhens live in houses built with logs. The Oroqens and Ewenkis put up their tents with some 30 tree branches in an umbrella shape, covered with birch bark or deerskin in winter. Others such as the Mongolian yurts, Tibetan carved houses, Dai bamboo houses, Hani mushroom shaped houses, Miao and Dong *Diaojiao* houses, Bouyei stone plate houses and Yi ship like houses are all built according to natural conditions and local custom. Some are mobile according to the needs of nomads, some serve the purposes of fire prevention, moisture proof or ventilation and some primarily maintain warmth. Aside from residences, Chinese minority people have constructed a number of magnificent buildings such as the Dong's drum towers and wood bridges with painted pavilions, Dai's bamboo-shoot towers, Tibetan monasteries, and mosques. They are treasures of world architecture.

Marriage composes a major part of social customs. Because of great differences in natural conditions, customs and habits, wedding ceremonies vary among different ethnic groups but primitive practices remain to a certain extent. As for the means of courtship, young men and women in different ethnic groups have their peculiar but effective methods. The common practices are antiphonal singing, throwing embroidered silk balls and singing at the doorstep of a woman's house. Bridal ceremonies are celebrated variously by different peoples. Some ride camels or horses, some meet the bride with a flamboyantly decorated sedan chair, some have the new couple cross a bridge made of a wooden board covered with the Chinese character "Xi", meaning happiness. Some share a bowl of wine and some twine white thread around the couple's wrists. Marriage by capture can be regarded as the most exciting and dramatic custom.

Funerals ceremonies vary from culture to culture. Burial, cremation, water burial, cliff burial, pagoda burial and exposure are common practices. Though the means of burial have a profound relation with local conditions, the varied funeral styles in some degree reflect the general ideas and values of the different peoples.

Of the 55 Chinese minority groups, each possesses traditional festivals of their own, totalling approximately one hundred. Some are closely related with agricultural production, some are religious and sacrificial, some festivals are only for a certain family, but most are get-togethers for several villages or regions. The number of participants varies from several hundreds to several thousands. No matter what the festival is, singing, dancing and sports competitions are essential for the celebration. During festivals, men and women, young and old all wear their rich attire and enjoy themselves for several days or even months. Today, as modern thoughts come gradually to the ethnic areas, people are able to have even happier and more prosperous festivals.

In China, nearly every minority group developed its own long history and splendid culture, which together make up the pluralistic civilization of the Chinese nation. Meanwhile, cultural exchange between the Hans and minorities has lasted for thousands of years. It is this friendly intermixing that has lain a solid foundation for a united multinational country and is a prominent feature of the Chinese culture.

In modern times, each group, including the Han, needs a peaceful environment for further development. Lets' use our intelligence and use all our efforts to work for a brighter future.

THE MONGOLIANS

The present population of the Mongolians numbers 4,806,849. Most of the China's Mongolians are living in the Inner Mongolian Autonomous Region, others are scattered in the Northeast and Northwest of China.

The Mongolians were legendary. In the past thousand years, they roamed over in the west, seeking rich pastures and water sources. Their traces can be easily founded in every corner of the vast pasture land of China.

Praised as "the divine son of the grassland", the Mongolian people also developed a high civilization. Especially since the Ming Dynasty, the Mongolians have contributed a lot to the development of China's science and culture in such aspects as history, literature, language, medicine, geography and astronomy. As regard to the folk arts, *Haolibao* is a popular singing form, while the Morin Hur is their traditional music instrument.

The Mongolians rose from the ancient Wangjian River (on the eastern bank of present Ergun River). As one of the Mongol tribes, they were called "Mongwu" in the Tang Dynasty. Early in the 13th century, Genghis Khan conquered other tribes on the grassland and unified them under Mongolian rule. Since then Mongolian have been known as a name of a nationality rather than a tribe.

The Mongolian language, including three dialects, the Inner, Mongolian, Weilate, and Barag-Buriat, forms a major branch of the Altaic language family.

CHINA'S MINORITY PEOPLES

6

7

8

9

1
The Inner Mongolian Autonomous Region is a vast pasture land where most people live by raising animals.
2
A Mongolian woman living in Erduos wearing her rich clothing.
3
Strong wrestlers.
4
A bird's-eye view of the *Nadam* Fair.
5
A foreign tourist and Mongolian wrestlers on the *Nadam* Fair.
6
Mongolian children practising wrestling.
7
Camels are major pack animals used by the Mongolians.
8
Mongolian women, living in Tonghai County of Yunnan Province, playing their traditional musical instrument called *Yueqin* whose full-moon-shaped sound box is decorated with elaborate carvings and small round mirrors.
9
The Morin Hur is a bowed stringed instrument with a scroll carved like a horse's head, used by the Mongolians.

THE HUIS

One of the largest minority groups in China is the Hui Nationality. Its population numbers 8,602,978. The largest Hui community is in Ningxia Hui Autonomous Region. A few live in Gansu, Qinghai, Hebei, Henan, Yunnan, Shandong and Xinjiang Autonomous Region.

Hui is short for Hui-Hui. The Huis have their roots in the Middle East. In the Tang and Song dynasties, a number of Arabian and Persian merchants came to China and settled down in the southeast coastal areas. They were called "Fanke" at that time. In the 13th century, the Mongolian army launched three Western Expeditions, forcing a large number of Moslems in the Central Asia to emigrate eastward to China. These immigrants, together with Fanke, intermarried with people of the same religion and occupations, and absorbed the customs of the Hans, Mongolians and Uygurs. Later this amalgamated group was called "Huihui".

Chinese is the common language of the Huis. However, in religious practices and social contacts, expressions from the Arabian and Persian languages are still in use. Those living in border areas adopted local languages.

The Hui people usually live in close-knit groups, but their communities scatter all parts of the country. In the interior of China, the Huis mainly live together with the Hans, while in border areas, they get along with other minority peoples. In most cases, the Hui settlements are built near traffic hubs, which enable the Hui people to develop a prosperous economy and a high culture.

The dress of the Huis looks the same as that of the Hans. The difference is headgear. Hui men wear white, black or brown caps. Women wear long head scarves. In the northwest areas, young women wear green head scarves, middle-aged women wear black or green, while old women wear white.

The Huis are Moslems. Islam played an important role in the forming of the Hui nationality.

The Huis were initially dependent for their livelihood on farming. Some raise animals or engage in handicraft. The Huis are outstanding businessmen. Their restaurants enjoy high fame.

1
During the Corban Festival, Moslems praying in the Tongxin Mosque.
2
White head scarves are only used by unmarried women.
3
A wedding of the Hui people.
4
A traditional sport among the Huis.

5
Sanzi is a fried wheaten food served during festivals.
6
Shearing sheep.
7
The Hui people living in the northwest love to wear embroidered earmuffs made of fox skin.

THE TIBETANS

The number of people of the Tibetan ancestry is placed at 4,593,330. They mainly live in Tibet Autonomous Region and the neighboring provinces such as Qinghai, Gansu, Sichuan and Yunnan.

Tibet, the roof of the world, is a land of mystery and home to one of China's most ancient ethnic groups -- the Tibetans. At present, Tibet Autonomous Region has more than 1.3 million inhabitants, 95% are Tibetans. In the Tibetan language, Tibet is called "Bo" and the Tibetans call themselves "Boba". But the name Tibetans use to call themselves differs from place to place. For example, those in Ngari use "Duiba", those in Shigatse use "Zangba", those in Lhasa use "Weiba", those in the west of Sichuan Province use "Kangba" and those in Qinghai, Yunnan, and northwest Sichuan provinces use "Anduowa".

The ancestors of Tibetans originally lived along the fertile banks of the Yarlung Zangbo River as early as the Qin and Han dynasties. The middle reaches of the river are an extremely rich area for pastoralism. The domestication of the hardy bovine creature, the yak, assured considerable wealth for Tibetan husbandmen. For yark can be used as pack animal and is a source of meat and butter. Sheep, goat, and pian niu (offspring of a bull and a female yak) are also important in the economy. Cereal, primarily *qingke* barley, is Tibet's staple crop and barley flour, called tsampa, forms the basic diet. Other crops are wheat, rape and pea.

The dress used by Tibetans, both men and women, is called *chuba*, and consists of a full gown with long sleeves that reach far below the fingertips. The style varies from place to place.

The Tibetan language, containing the Weizang, Kang and Anduo dialects, belongs to the Tibeto-Burmar group of the Sino-Tibetan family. The use of the Tibetan language strengthened the economic ties with the Central Plains of China. In 641, the Tibetan king Songzen Gampo married Princess Wen Cheng of the Tang Dynasty. This event brought about an unprecedented development in the Tibetan culture. From the 10th to 16th centuries, Tibetan civilization reached its zenith in the publication of the two voluminous Buddhist encyclopedic works the *Kanjur* and *Tenjur*. Moreover, a wealth of treatises in prosody, literature, philosophy, history, geography, astronomy, calendar and medicine came out in this period.

The Tibetans are by nature ebullient, sanguine and bold, so are their folk arts. A very popular art form in Tibet is the dance drama. Dancers move their body with sprightly rhythm singing pleasant lyrics.

Buddhism probably first entered Tibet in the 4th century A.D. from Kashmis and Nepal. It was adopted as the court religion in the 7th century. From the 13th to the mid-16th centuries, Buddhism became popular. Monastic system spread widely throught Tibet, finally emerging as the predominant religious institute. The most famous monasteries are Ganden, Sera, Drepung, Tashi Lhunpo and the Potala Palace.

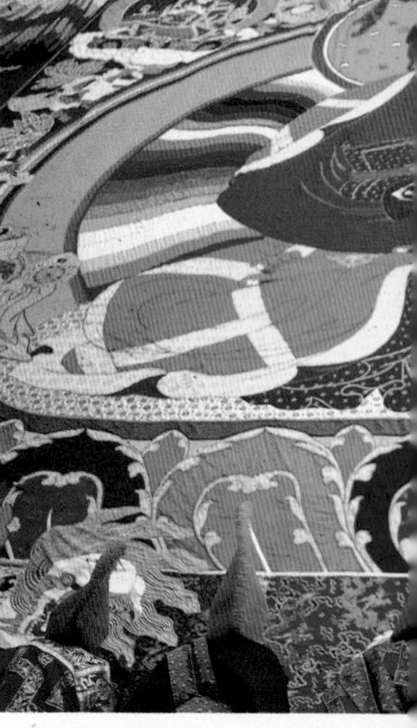

1
The magnificent Potala Palace on the Red Hill in Lhasa, Tibet.
2
A huge picture of Buddha made of silk.
3
During the Buddhist Worship Festival, lamas of the Tashi Lhunpo Monastery sprinkle holy water on a bronze mirror to pay their devotion to the Buddha.
4
Lamas are blowing the huge Buddhist horns. The Buddhist Worship Festival is started.
5
Tibetan women living in Ngari love to wear gems, agate, and emeralds in their plaits and on chest.
6
Every early morning, many Buddhists come to worship the figures of Buddha carved on the cliffs of the Yaowang Mountain, Lhasa.

7
Tibetan Embroideries.
8
An equestrian event.
9
Tibetan women living in Yushu of Qinghai Province love to wear silver shields on their back.
10
Kang Rimpoche and Mapam Yunco are worshipped as the holy mountain and lake by the Tibetans. Every Summer and Autumn, a great number of pious Buddhists come to bathe in the lake, then bring the clear water bake home and send it as valuable present to their friends and relatives.
11
A Tibetan craftsman.
12
Tibet produces and sells nice hand-made carpets.
13
A Tibetan girl is surrounded by a pack of dogs.

10

12

11

13

THE UYGURS

In the northwest border area and in the foothills of the snowcapped Tianshan Mountains lives an ebullient people — the Uygurs. Its population is 7,214,431. According to historical sources, ancestry of the Uygurs can be traced to a nomadic group of the third century A.D. in the areas between the Ertix River and the Barkeshi Lake and in the south of the Baikal Lake. Suffered from unceasing tribal warfare, many nomads moved to present Xinjiang, called the Western Regions at that time. In history, they were successively called the Weiho, Wuhe, Yuanhe, Huigu or Weiwuerh people. Later, they took the name Uygur meaning "unity" or "alliance".

The Uygurs mainly engage in farming. They grow cotton, wheat, maize, and rice, and excel in horticulture. The Grape Valley, the largest grapes production base of China, is located in Turpan, 184 kilometers southeast of Urumchi, the capital city of Xingjiang Autonomous Region.

The Uygurs are Moslems and have their own language and systems of writing. The most important religious festivals are the Corban, Lasser Bairam, and Nuoluzi.

Singing and dancing are improtant parts of the Uygurs' cultural life. The *Twelve Mukamu* is a popular ancient musical epic, which makes up a brilliant part of the Uygur culture. Uygur dances are fast and complicated. The most enjoyable are the bowl, plate and tambourine dances.

1
Uygur children during the grape festival.
2
Standing in Kashi of Xinjiang, the 140-year-old Id Kah Mosque is built in an ethnic style. The magnificent mosque can house 7,000 Moslems at the same time.
3
Airing grapes to make raisin.

4
Xinjiang Uygur Autonomous Region is noted for sweet Hami melons.
5
The traditional Chicken Dance.
6
The Uygurs have several dozne traditional musical instruments, most of which are plucked.
7
Uygur farmers living in the Grape Valley of Turpan often entertain their guests under grape trellis.
8
A Uygur old man.

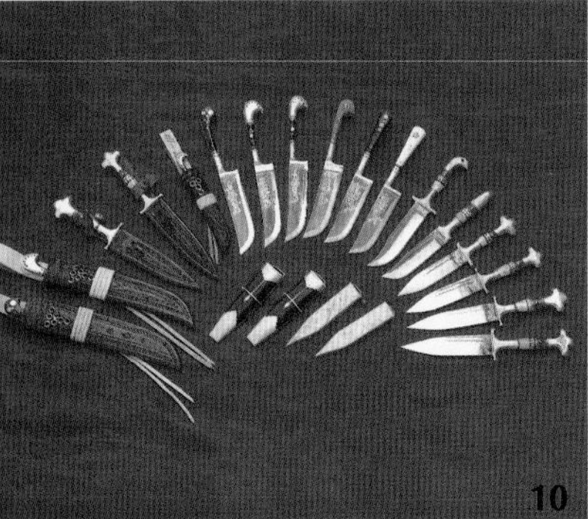

9
Delicious kebabs.
10
Yengisar knives.
11
Embroidered caps.

THE MIAOS

The Miaos, with a population of 7,398,035, are mainly distributed in Guizhou, Hunan, Yunnan provinces and the Guangxi Zhuang Autonomous Region.

On the flatland of the warm and rainy Miaoling and Wuling mountains, the Miaos grow rice, maize, wheat, cotton, tobacco, millet, rape, and tung trees. The mountain areas where the Miaos make their homes also have abundant timber and mineral resources.

The present Miao people can be traded back to the primitive Chi You Tribe living in the Central Plains several thousand years ago. In the Shang and Zhou periods, forefathers of the Miaos established the Three-Miaos State in the middle and lower reaches of the Changjiang River planting rice for food. For some reasons, these people had moved for several times. The migrating route was approximately from the Yellow River Valley, to Hunan, Guizhou and Yunnan.

The Miao language belongs to the Miao-Yao group in the Sino-Tibetan family. Formerly, the Miao people had no script. Later, in the 1950s, a Romanization system for the Miao language was created. At present, most Miao people use Chinese.

The Miao songs and dances have a long history. The complicated Reed Pipe Dance is very popular. Their cross-stitch work, embroidery, batiks, brocades and ornaments are exquisite folk arts and enjoy high fame. The Miaos have many festivals. The most important are the New Year's Day of the Miaos, the Eighth Day of the Fifth Month of lunar year, and the Dragon-boat Festival.

1

1
Once a girl is born to a Miao family, her parents will start to save money for their daughter to make silver ornaments. A complete set of silver ornaments normally weighs several kilograms. The picture shows Miao women sharing multicolored glutinous rice on the Sisters' Day.

2
When a guest comes to a Miao village, he must empty the block-the-way wine before he is invited to their houses.

3
Decking up in holiday array.
4
A Miao woman living in Xiangxi of Hunan Province.
5
Miao people living in Rongshui of Guangxi celebrate their festivals with the Reed Pipe Dance.
6
The scarecrow dance.
7
Miao women, living in Zhijin of Guizhou Province, dress their hair up with black knitting wool to form a supper large coiffure.
8
Miao men, living in Zhaotong Prefecture of Yunnan Province gather to play reed pipes in their bright-colored clothing.
9
A young man living in the Wumeng mountain area in his rich Miao attire.
10
Hua Miao children, living in Anshun, Guizhou Province, and their dress.

6

CHINA'S MINORITY PEOPLES

10

7

8

11
Miao women living in Zhijin, Guizhou Province.
12
Miao women, living in Rongshui, Guangxi, and their ornaments.
13
Miao women, living in Anning, Yunnan Province, and their ornaments.

THE YIS

With a population of 6,572,173, the Yi Nationality is one of the oldest minority groups in the southwest of China, mostly concentrated in the mountain areas of Yunnan, Sichuan, Guizhou provinces and the northeast of Guangxi Zhuang Autonomous Region. Meandering rivers, deep valleys, ripply lakes and rich flatland altogether make the Yi areas look like fairylands.

The Yi people has many branches. They called themselves variously such as "Nuosu", "Nasu", and "Niesu". The name of Yi Nationality was generally accepted after the founding of new China.

The Yis used a solar calendar in old days. Most of them plant crops and some raise animals. The Yi language, containing 6 dialects, belongs to the Tibeto-Burmar group of the Sino-Tibetan family. The syllabic Yi script is still in use. Many valuable works in history, literature, medicine and folk tales are written in the Yi language. Music of the Yi people is unique and the people love to sing and dance. Traditional silver ornaments, embroidery, lacquer painting, carvings and paintings of the Yis are full of folk features.

1

Yi women in new dress.

2

An amusing wedding of the Huayao Yi people living in Yuxi Prefecture.

3

Nasu Yi women threshing corn.

6

5

9
Yi women of Honghe Prefecture and their clothing.
10
Yi women of Chuxiong Prefecture, Yunnan Province, in their ethnic clothes.
11
The Yis, living in Daliang Mountain area, and their houses.

4
Yi women of Weishan County, Yunnan Province wear colorful clothes. Their most prominent mark is the round ornament made of felt hanging at waist.
5
In the first month of a lunar year, Yi people, living in Lufeng County, Yunnan Province, celebrate their Broadsword Festival, which more or less resembles the Hans' *Shehuo*, a religious festival with art performance to sacrifice to God of land. The Yis, with their face painted and broadswords in hand, parade for a good harvest in the coming year.
6
Normally, the Torch Festival, the most important to the Yis, begins with a mountain horn performance.
7
When the night falls during the Torch Festival, Yi people gather in the field, torches in hands, to exorcise evils and pray for fortune.
8
Wearing their ethnic clothing, Yi people, living in Yunnan Province, blowing gourd pipes during the Torch Festival.

THE ZHUANGS

Of China's minority groups, the Zhuang Nationality is the largest, with a population of 15,489,630. They mostly inhabit Guangxi Zhuang Autonomous Region, and some are distributed in Guangdong, Guizhou, Yunnan and Hunan provinces.

The Zhuangs are the aborigines of the Lingnan area. West of Lingnan is a land of great natural beauty with unique and charming karst terrain. Moistened by the mild climate and plentiful rainfall, tropical and subtropical plants abound. The staples are rice, maize and potato. Pseudo-ginseng, gecko and fennel oil are world famous products.

In history, the Zhuangs were variously called the Buzhuang, Butu, Bunong, Buman or Buyayi people. After the founding of new China, they were generally called the Tong Nationality. Later they took the name Zhuang.

The Zhuang language belongs to the Dai branch of Zhuang-Dong Group of the Sino-Tibetan family. The ancient Zhuang script was created by imitating the regulations of *the Six Categories of Chinese Characters*. Since the 1950s, an acceptable syllabic writing system has been put into use in line with their requirement.

3

7

5

6

8

1
A Zhuang maiden is going to throw her embroidered silk ball to her boy friend.
2
The Zhuang pony, about 1 meter high, is nimble, docile and suitable for children to ride.
3
A good harvest of sugarcane.
4
Zhuang women are good at making rattan chairs.
5
A part of the cliff paintings in the Huashan Mountain.
6
The Zhuang brocade.
7
The Paper Horse Dance is traditional among the Zhuangs. In the past, they used paper horses in the dance. But now, colorful silk is used to make abstract figures.
8
The third day of the third month in the lunar year is the Song Festival of the Zhuangs.

THE BOUYEIS

5

The population of the Bouyei Nationality is 2,545,059. Most of the Bouyei people live in Qiannan and Qianxinan Bouyei-Miao autonomous prefectures and Duyun, Dushan, Pingtang and Zhenning counties ofGuizhou Province. Others live scattered in Yunnan, Sichuan and Guangxi.

The Bouyei area boasts dramatic landscape. There are a dozen of scenic spots in this area, which receive thousands of tourists from all over the world each year. The most famous are the Huangguoshu Waterfalls, Huaxi in Guiyang, the Dragon Palace Cave in Anshun and the Chain Bridge over the Panjiang River. This area also abounds in wild plants, animals and mineral resources.

The Bouyei people have a long history in growing rice. The Honghe River Basin is one of the largest forest areas of China.

As early as the Stone Age, Bouyei people made their homes in the southeast of the Yunnan-Guizhou Plateau and were closely related to the ancient Liao, Baiyue and Baipu peoples. The Tang government called them "Xinanman". In the Song and Yuan dynasties, they were known as the Fan or Zhongjiaman people and were called the Zhongmans in the Ming and Qing dynasties. Since the founding of the People's Republic of China, these mountaineers have been generally called the Bouyei Nationality.

The Bouyei language belongs to the Zhuang-Dai branch of the Zhuang-Dong Group of the Sino-Tibetan family. No writing system was created until the 1950s. However, this system was not acceptable to most of the Bouyeis. Now they generally use Chinese.

1

1
Bouyei women, living in Zhenning, Guizhou Province, rinsing their batiks by the famous Huangguoshu Waterfalls.
2
Bouyei women performing the Bench Dance.
3
The percussion band of a Bouyei Opera Troupe.
4
A stone house of Bouyei people.
5
Bouyei women, living in Qianxinan Prefecture, Guizhou Province, love to wear large turbans.

3

THE KOREANS

Most of the Korean people, numbering 1,920,597, live in Jilin, Heilongjiang and Liaoning provinces. Others live scattered in Inner Mongolia Autonomous Region. The largest Korean community is in Yanbian Autonomous Prefecture.

Three hundred years ago, ancestors of the Korean people moved from the Korean Peninsula to the Northeast of China. They have their own language and writing system. However, their language was variously considered. Most of the Chinese linguists incline that it belongs to the Altaic language family.

The Koreans are mainly engaged in farming. They know how to grow rice in a cold climate, and have turned Yanbian Prefecture into a major rice producer in the Northeast of China after years of hard work.

2

1

A Korean wedding. The groom's family prepared a lot of delicious food to entertain the bride, bridesmaids and guests.

2

Springboard is a traditional competition among the Koreans.

3

The ethnic panoply of Korean women.

4

The Korean area teems with red pepper, which adds more flavor to their cuisine.

5

The long drum, a Korean percussion instrument, looks like a cylinder with a solid middle part and two hollow ends. On festivals, Korean women dance while beating long drums. This is what they call the Long Drum Dance.

2

THE MANCHUS

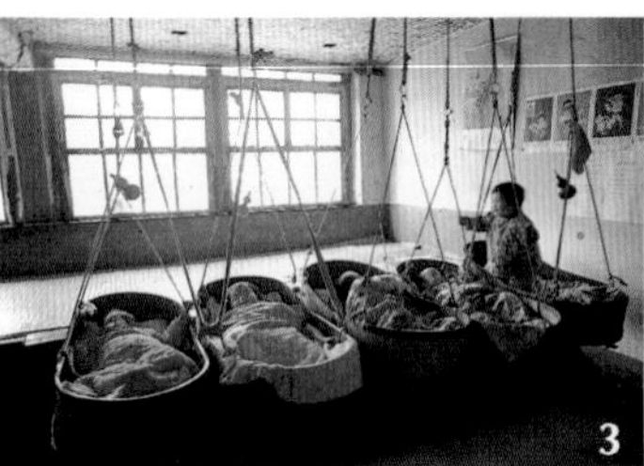
3

4

The present population of the Manchu Nationality is 9,821,180. Most of the Manchu people live in the Northeast of China. The largest Manchu community lies in Liaoning Province. Others are widely distributed in cities throughout China.

The Manchu Nationality has an extremely long history. The Sushen people, living 2,000 years ago, was their earliest ancestors. They were called the Yilous in the Han Dynasty, the Wujis in the Southern and Northern dynasties, the Mohos in the Sui and Tang dynasties and the Jurchens in the Liao, Song, Yuan and Ming periods. In ancient times, these people roamed in the east of the Changbai Mountain and the Heilong and Wusuli river valleys. In the late 16th century; the Jurchens led by Nurhachi and emerged as excellent horsemen and skilled mounted archers, amalgamated some Han, Mongolian and Korean people. Later, a new community — the Manchus came into being.

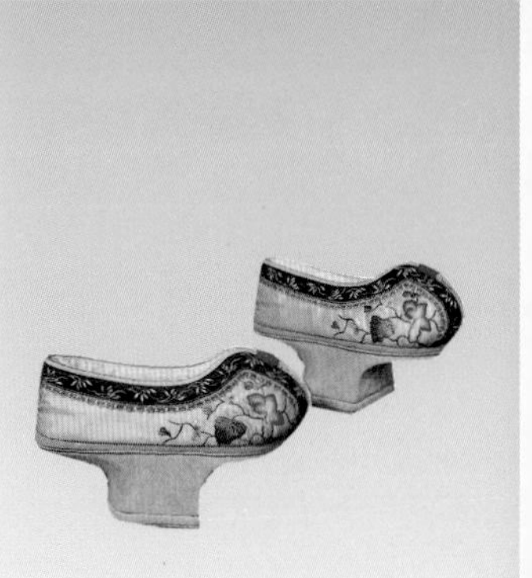

7

The Manchus have their own oral and written language. It belongs to the Manchu-Tungusic group in the Altaic language family. The writing system, created towards the end of the 16th century, adopted the Mongolian alphabet, to which dots and circles were added. After the Manchus unified the country under their Qing Dynasty, a large number of Manchu people moved to the Central Plains. To better contact with the Hans both in economy and culture, many Manchu people learnt to speak Chinese.

Today, most Manchu people are farmers. Those living in cities work in industrial and cultural enterprises. For centuries, the Manchu people have made immortal contribution to the formation of the Chinese nation and the development of Chinese culture.

1

1
Whenever there was a ceremony in the court of the Qing Dynasty, the Manchu Peace Drum Dance must be served. Today, people can often see this traditional dance on the stage.
2
At a Manchu wedding ceremony, the bride hides behind a red kerchief. When the couple steps into the bridal chamber, the bridegroom firstly lifts the veil with a horsewhip and tosses it onto the roof.
3
Manchu cradles.
4
A shop selling Manchu clothing.
5
Paper-cut.
6
The traditional dress of Manchu women.
7
The horse-hoof shoes of Manchu noblewomen of the Qing Dynasty.

5

THE DONGS

The Dong people, with a population of 2,514,014, make their homes in Qiandongnan, Yuping, Xinhuang, Tongdao, Zhijiang and Sanjiang counties where Guizhou, Hunan provinces and the Guangxi Zhuang Autonomous Region meet.

Dong people are excellent farmers. They plant rice and breed fish in paddy. A small number cultivate trees. The Dongs grow delicious glutinous rice, the best-known is the Xianghe glutinous rice.

The Dong people were known as the Yilings in the historical documents of the Song Dynasty. Later in the Ming and Qing dynasties, they were variously called "Dongman", "Dongmiao", "Dongren" or "Dongjia". After the founding of the People's Republic of China, these people were formally named the Dong Nationality, but folks prefer Dongjia.

The Dong language belongs to the Dong-Shui branch of the Zhuang-Dong group of the Sino-Tibetan family. It had no written form until the 1950s. But most Dong people now use Chinese.

The Dongs say that every one of them can sing and improvise lyrics. Dong songs have strict rules of rhyming, but people manage to express whatever they see and feel quite easily. The most splendid is the traditional *Dage*, normally sung a cappella with many parts. It possesses great value both in literature and music.

The Dongs are especially skilled in building bridges and in Dong territory exquisite drum towers and wood bridges with painted pavilions are common and represent the achievements of the Dong architecture. Many Dong people can also do silk embroidery, cross-stitch work, silver ornaments and weave elaborate cloth and brocade.

1

3

2

4

1
Singing and dancing during festivals.

2
The Dongs' *Dage* is normally sung together by men and women in several parts.

3
Oil tea is the Dongs' favorite food.

4
Dong people welcome their honored guests by putting road-blocks in front of their village. Every guest must empty a bowl of glutinous rice wine before his entrance.

5
The Dongs' embroidered tiger-shaped pillows.

1

THE YAOS

The Yaos, with a population of 2,134,013, are mainly distributed in Guangxi, Hunan, Yunnan, Guangdong, Guizhou and Jiangxi provinces.

Ancestors of the Yao people formerly inhabited the Changjiang River Basin. During the Qin and Han dynasties, they formed a part of the Changsha Wulingmans, also called the Wuximans. When these people moved southward, some tribes settled down in the southwest mountain areas. It is said that every peak of the Nanling Mountains is inhabited by Yaos.

The Yao people have their homes in subtropical mountain areas about 1,000 to 2,000 meters above sea level. Yao villages are usually surrounded by thick bamboo and trees. Different Yao tribes used to have different names in accordance with their tribal origins, occupations, attire and custom. Hence there were more than 20 branches among the Yao people such as the Pan Yao, Chashan Yao, Shanzi Yao, Ao Yao, Hualan Yao, Baiku Yao and Hongtou Yao. After the founding of new China, they were given a single appellation.

The Yao language belongs to the Miao-Yao group of the Sino-Tibetan family. Owing to centuries of contact with the Hans, Miaos and Zhuangs, many Yao people speak the Chinese, Zhuang and Miao languages.

Living in solitary mountains, most Yao people lead a primitive life, simply farming, hunting and fishing. Even in modern days, the Yaos still retain their ancient folk tales, beautiful songs, quaint dances, unique marriage, and faith. Yao women are noted for making elaborate brocade and colorful clothing.

2

1
The Yaos, living in Jinping of Yunnan Province, wear large red turbans. So they are also called the Hongtou (Red Turban) Yaos.
2
A wedding of the Yaos living in Jinxiu, Yunnan Province. The bride and groom undergo the kneeling rituals in the ceremonial hall.
3
The traditional Bieh Hungh Festival.
4
The Yaos celebrate the Bieh Huangh Festival with the Huangni Drum Dance.
5
The Beneficence Festival is traditional among the Yaos living in Jinxiu. During this religious festival, people not only repair their bridges, but also worship Bodhisattvas with the Beneficence Dance.
6
In the past, a bronze drum was the symbol of right among the Baiku (White Breeches) Yaos. It could only be beaten by tribe leaders. But now, during festivals and at ceremonies, a dozen of bronze drums, accompanied by leather drums, sound simultaneously. What an exciting scene!
7
Shanzi Yao young boys, living in Dayao Mountains of Jinxiu, are normally accepted as adults at the age of 15, when they begin to receive trust and respect from the community. A special rite is held to approve their adulthood. Firstly the young men cover their faces with masks and sacrifice roosters to their ancestors. Later, these young men must overcome great odds and ends before they are fully qualified to participate all the tribal activities.
8
Houses built by the Chashan (Tea Hill) Yao people living in Dayao Mountains.

THE BAIS

In China, there are 1,594,827 people of the Bai nationality. Most of them reside around the Ehai Lake in the Dali Bai Autonomous Prefecture in the west of Yunnan Province. The rest live elsewhere in Sichuan, Guizhou and Hunan provinces.

At the foot of the snowcapped Cangshan Mountain and by the clear blue Ehai Lake is the world famous Dali City where the Bais have long inhabited.

The Bai areas enjoy prosperous economy and high civilization. Stable Bai communities have come into being from time immemorial. In the Han and Jin dynasties, the Bais' ancestors were called "Kunming". The Tang government called them "Heman", "Songwaiman" or "Baiman", while in the Yuan and Ming dynasties, they were known as the Bos. The Bai people showed special interests in white color. Hence, the name of Bai Nationality was generally accepted by them after the founding of new China.

The Bai language belongs to the Tibeto-Burman group of the Sino-Tibetan family. Most Bai people speak Chinese, through which they communicate with other nationalities.

As an ancient ethnic group, the Bais are proud of their splendid civilization. In old days, Bai scholars were pioneers in astronomy, meteorology, medicine, painting and literature, and left a wealth of valuable cultural treasures such as the three pagodas in Chongsheng Temple of Dali, grottoes in Shibao Mountain of Jianchuan, the picture roll of the history of Nanzhao Zhongxing Kingdom and the picture roll of Dali.

The Bais have long been an agricultural people. They till the earth and fish as well. Today, the Bai area has been developed into a major grain and fish producer in the southwest border region.

1
The Three Pagodas in Dali City.
2
Bai women.
3
The Third Month Street Fair is the principal festival of the Bais.
4
The padauk furniture.
5
The gate tower forms an important part of the Bais' residence.
6
Bai Children.
7
A Bai bride in her rich phoenix headdress.
8
The dowry.

4

5

6

8

7

THE HANIS

Today, a great majority of the Hani people, numbering 1,253,952, live between the Honghe and Lancang rivers in the south of Yunnan Province. Others are distributed in Pu'er, Menghai, Jinghong, Mengla, Luquan and Xinping.

In history, the Hanis called themselves variously such as "Hani", "Kaduo", "Aini", "Haoni", "Biyue", "Budu" or "Baihong". After the founding of new China, they were generally called the Hani Nationality.

The Hani language belongs to the Yi language branch of the Tibeto-Burman group of the Sino-Tibetan family. This oral language contains 3 dialects — the Hani, Bika and Haobai. In the 1950s, an alphabetic writing system was created, but it aborted.

Most Hani people live on the level tops of mountains about 800 to 2,500 meters above sea level. They build terraced fields that climb from the valley bottom to the mountain top, irrigated by water piped from rivers and streams. Mojiang produces the most shellac in China.

Hani people worship natural god and their ancestors. Rich folk tales are left. In Hani villages, men and women, young and old always keep their favorite musical instruments at hand. A Hani New Year begins in the 10th lunar month, and their festivals include the Tenth Month Festival and Sixth Month Festival (Kuzhazha), also known as the field worshipping festival.

1
The Hanis celebrate their new year's day with a grand feast in the middle of the village street.
2
The Bamboo Tube Dance.
3
Hani women, living in Lancang County, rubbing tea.
4
Hani women are diligent. On their way to the field, they often skein and never rest their hands.
5
Yeche (a branch of the Hanis) women, living in the Ailao Mountain area.
6
Husking glutinous rice.
7
A Hani woman, living in Xishuangbanna Prefecture, and her attire.

3

4

5

6

7

THE KAZAKS

The Kazaks, with a population of 1,111,718, mostly live in Ili Kazak Autonomous Prefecture, Mori and Barkol Kazak Autonomous Counties. The rest are distributed in Gansu and Qinghai provinces.

Located in the north of Xinjiang Autonomous Region, the Kazak communities are surrounded by the Tianshan, Altay and Tarbagatay mountains. In the middle are the Junggar and Ili basins with the Ili, Tekes, Emin, Ertix and Wulungu rivers winding through and alpine lakes rippling on top of mountains. In winter, the weather is extremely cold, while in summer it's cool with dramatic nighttime drops in temperature. Therefore, the Kazaks drive their cattle, horses, and sheep each year alternately from sunny slopes on the edge of the basins in summers and then back to the river valleys in winters. There was very little farming and few trade. However, with the rapid growth of the socialist market economy, many Kazak people have become successful businessmen.

The history of Kazak people can be traced back to the Wusuns in the Western Han Dynasty. The Kazaks emerged in the mid-15th century as a distinctive ethnic community, an amalgam of various Turkic speaking nomads. The dominant strain in this amalgam was provided by the ancient Kipchak people. According to a folk myth, the word Kazak means "warrior" or "white swan", who were believed as progenitors of the Kazaks.

The Kazaks are Moslems. The Kazak language belongs to the Turkic group of the Altaic family. In ancient times, the Kazkas spoke the Turkic and Huihu languages. Now the written form of the Kazak language is based on Arabic letters.

Ili is the hometown of Ili steeds, Xinjiang fine-wool sheep and Altay sheep. The Kazaks eat a lot of meat. Sausage made of horse meat is their unique food and Koumiss is the favorite drink in summer. The Kazaks love horse sports. Sheep snatching, horse racing and the girl chase are the traditional games on horseback.

Throughout their history, a wealth of ancient poems, tales, maxims and proverbs passed on from generation to generation. Story-tellers among the Kazak people are called Aken. They tour about and sing the legends of their proud ancestors for folks. Dances and songs of the Kazaks are sprightly. The traditional folk musical instrument *Dongbula* makes rich melodies.

1
The Girl Chase is a very popular game among the Kazak people.
2
Kazak women and children can be easily distinguished from other ethnic groups because there is a tuft of feather sewn on their embroidered hats.
3
A story-singer is called "Aken" by the Kazak people.
4
Move to another pasture during changes of season.
5
A Kazak wedding.

1

3

4

THE TUJIAS

1
A beautiful Tujia woman.
2
A Tujia wedding.
3
The Tujias are noted for their *Maogusi* dance.
4
Tujia women celebrating the Spring Festival.

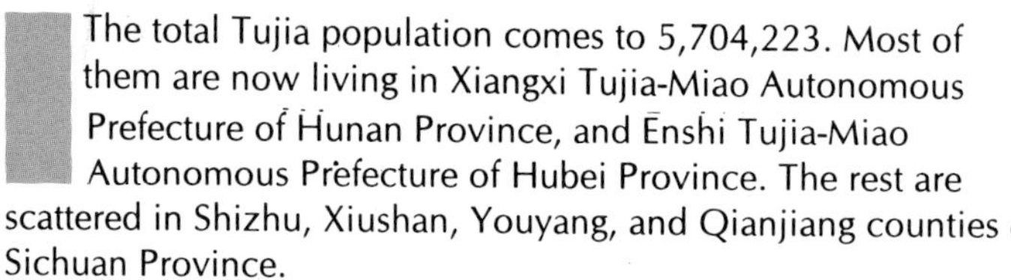

The total Tujia population comes to 5,704,223. Most of them are now living in Xiangxi Tujia-Miao Autonomous Prefecture of Hunan Province, and Enshi Tujia-Miao Autonomous Prefecture of Hubei Province. The rest are scattered in Shizhu, Xiushan, Youyang, and Qianjiang counties of Sichuan Province.

The hilly Tujia area is known for rich resources, great natural beauty, and distinctive folk tradition. Zhangjiajie, the first national forest park, is located in this area and has been built into a new tourist attraction.

The Tujias call themselves "Bizica", meaning "aborigines". About 2,000 years ago, their ancestors settled down in the hills in the west of Hunan and Hubei provinces and were called "Wulingman" or "Wuximan" together with other minority peoples. After the Song Dynasty, they were known as the Tuding or Tumin people. After the founding of new China, they were officially called the Tujia Nationality with their approval.

The Tujia language belongs to the Tibeto-Burman group of the Sino-Tibetan family. Tujia people have long lived together with the Hans, and many Tujia people learnt to speak and write Chinese in a fairly early time. Only in a few areas such as Longshan, Yongshun and Guzhang counties, Tujia language still can be heard.

Under Han influence, Tujia's farming economy and culture quickly developed, but their traditions remained. The golden tung oil made in the west of Hunan Province and lacquer made in the west of Hubei are world famous products.

THE DAIS

The Dai nationality has a population of 1,025,128 living close together in Xishuangbanna Dai Autonomous Prefecture, Dehong Dai-Jingpo Autonomous Prefecture and Gengma, Menglian, Yuanjiang and Xinping autonomous counties in the west of Yunnan Province.

The Dai area is located in the west of the Yunnan-Guizhou Plateau with Gaoligong, Nushan and Ailao mountains as its natural defence. The swift currents of Lancang, Nujiang and Yuanjiang rivers rush through the deep valleys. On the plateau, there are many endowed small plains, where the Dais make their homes. The plains are fertile, and yielding an abundance of tropical and subtropical crops and rare medicinal herbs. The Dai's staple is rice. Today, Xishuangbanna and Dehong are praised as the granaries of southern Yunnan.

The Dai people has a long history. Their ancestors were called "Dianyue" in the Han Dynasty, "Pu", "Yue", or "Liao" in the Wei and Jin dynasties, "Jinchi", "Yichi" and "Baiyi" in the Tang and Song dynasties, and "Baiyi" in the Qing Dynasty. After the founding of new China, they were named the Dai Nationality according to their own wishes.

The Dai language belongs to the Zhuang-Dai branch of the Zhuang-Dong group of the Sino-Tibetan family. In different areas, four kinds of writing systems including Daili, Daina, Daibeng and Daiduan are still in use. These written forms came from India alphabet. As shapes of these letters have changed a lot, linguists classify these writing systems as variants of Sanskrit of the Indo-China Peninsula system. Throughout their history, the Dai people kept a record of their culture and history through these letters.

There are 3 branches among the Dai people. They are the Water Dai, Dry Dai and Huayao Dai. Each branch has their traditional attire. The most valuable for research are the Huayao attire in Xinping and the Jinping attire of the Qing Dynasty.

1
A group of pagodas in Xishuangbanna.
2
After their daily lessons, little Dai monks are allowed to go to a fair.

3
The Water Splashing Festival celebrates the Dais' New Year.
4
The baby elephant is a pet of these Dai children.
5
Dai women, living in Chuxiong Prefecture, Yunnan Province, love to wear colorful girdles. Hence these people are called the Huayao (colorful girdle) Dais.
6
There is a distict diversity of clothing between the Dai women living in Chuxiong

Prefecture and those living in Xishuangbanna, but they share almost the same customs and faiths.

7
"A cast of ball" is a romantic Dai game among the unmarried youths. It may sometimes be the precursor to a union of love.

8
The attire of the Huayao Dais looks gorgeous. The jacket made of silk is fully decorated with silver bells and tassels.

9
A Dai wedding ceremony.

THE LIS

The Li population comes to 1,110,900. Most of the Lis now live in Dongfang, Baisha, Lingshui, Changjiang Li Autonomous Counties, and Ledong, Qiongzhong, and Baoting Li-Miao Autonomous Counties in the middle south of Hainan Province. The rest are scattered elsewhere in cities of the island or live together with other nationalities.

The Wuzhi Mountain area where the Lis make their homes is in the picturesque subtropical zones. The long summer makes it possible to harvest rice crops three times a year. This beautiful land attracts more and more tourists each year.

Rice is the staple crop of the Lis. In addition to farming, local people developed a diversified economy, fishing, hunting, gathering and planting trees.

According to archeologists, the Lis are the earliest inhabitants of the fertile Hainan Island. The primitive cultural relics of the New Stone Age left by the Li progenitors are over 100. The Lis were developed from the ancient Yue people and had close origins with the Luoyue people, which was a branch of the Baiyue group. In history, the Lis called themselves "Xiao", "Qi", "Bendi", "Meifu" or "Sai". After the Song Dynasty, they took the name Li.

The Li language belongs to the Zhuang-Dong group of the Sino-Tibetan family and has no script. After the founding of new China, the Lis started to use Chinese.

1
Li children.
2
Young people performing the Bamboo Dance on the Lis' Third Month Street Fair, which is celebrated on the third day of the third moon of the lunar calendar.
3
A Li thatched cottage.
4
Weaving a straight skirt.

THE LISUS

1
The *Sanxuan* Dance performance during the Lisus' *Daogan* Festival.
2
Sharing a bowl of wine side by side with intimates is a local custom.
3
A Lisu woman.
4
Burying her boyfriend with river sand is a popular courting game among the Lisu youths.
5
Climbing a ladder made of knives on bare feet.

The Lisu population is 574,856. Most of the Lisus now live in Bijiang, Fugong, Gongshan and Lushui counties of Nujiang Lisu Autonomous Prefecture, north of Yunnan Province. The rest live together with the Hans, Bais, Yis and Naxis in the neighboring Tengchong and the adjoining area to Sichuan Province.

In the eighth century, ancestors of the Lisus inhabited the banks of the Jinsha River. In the mid-16th century, they moved to the Nujiang River Valley. Between the 17th to 18th centuries, a great number of Lisu people migrated to Dehong, Lincang and Gengma of Yunnan Province. Some made their homes in Lüquan and Dayao in the southern part of the Jinsha River Valley.

The Lisu language belongs to the Tibeto-Burman group of the Sino-Tibetan family. Its written form was not quite complete. After 1957, a Romanization writing became prevalent.

The Lisu villages are distributed in the two north-to-south gorges eroded by the swift currents of the Nujiang and Lancang rivers. This area has abundant mineral and hydropower resources and produces rare fur and mountain products.

The Lisu people are noted for their frank and hospitable personality. Their festivals resemble those of the neighboring Hans, Bais and Nanxis. The New Year's Day is the first day of a lunar year. The Torch and Harvest festivals fall in June and October respectively.

THE VAS

The Va population is 351,974. They make their homes in Ximeng, Cangyuan, Menglian, and Gengma counties in the southwest of Yunnan Province.

The Va area, located in the southern foothills of the Nushan Mountains and between the Lanchang and Sarun rivers, is called the Awa Mountain Region. This solitary area with few flatland has a complicate climate, but yields abundant of cash plants and is an ideal home of many rare wild animals such as tiger, leopard, bear, wild boar, and roe deer.

The Vas call themselves Awa. In the Zhou and Qin dynasties, they made up a branch of Baipu. Later in the Qing Dynasty, they were called "Gala", "Hawa" or "Kawa". Since the founding of new China, they have been generally called the Va Nationality, meaning "mountaineers".

The Va language belongs to the Austro-Asiatic family. It had no written script until the 1950s. Throughout their history, the Vas kept records by making notches on wood.

The Vas basically rely on farming. They love drinking and chewing betel nuts that tint their teeth black and lips red. The Vas drink with bamboo tubes. Whenever there is a festival, wedding, funeral, reception or discussion, wine must be served according to the traditional rites. Hence the saying goes that there's no ceremony without wine.

The Vas are good singers and dancers. The most popular are the Circle Dance and the Mortar & Pestle Dance. When the Circle Dance starts, people, no matter men or women, young or old, dance and sing hand in hand with sprightly rhythm.
dance and sing hand in hand with the cheerful rhythm.

1
The Va Wooden Drum Dance.
2
Husking rice with mortar and pestle.
3
The traditional dress of Ximeng Va women.
4
Old Va women love to wear big hollow earrings, in which they put money when they go to a fair.

THE SHES

The Shes, with a population of 630,378, mainly live in the mountainous areas of Fujian and Zhejiang provinces. A few are distributed in Jiangxi, Guangdong and Anhui provinces. A She village usually contains less than 100 families, and many families are assimilated with the Hans.

Located in the southeast, the hilly She area, with small rivers winding about, is productive and reserves rich resources. Thanks to the humid climate, the land is suitable for many varieties of crops. The most famous products are the Jingning Xianggu mushroom and Huiming tea.

As early as the Tang Dynasty, the Shes made their homes in the place where Fujian, Guangdong and Jiangxi provinces meet. In the historical documents of the Southern Song Dynasty, they were called the She people. However, the Shes called themselves "Shanha" or "Shanda" meaning "mountain guests". After the founding of new China, they were generally called the She Nationality.

The She language belongs to the Sino-Tibetan family, but most of the She people speak local dialects. As the She language has no script, they use Chinese.

A She wedding ceremony.

Young men and women court with antiphonal singing.

A She family.

Ornaments and embroidered silk balls.

THE GAOSHANS

The Gaoshan population is 400,000. Most of them live in Taiwan Province. About 3,000 are scattered in the coastal area of Fujian and Zhejiang provinces.

There are nine branches among the Gaoshans including the Amei, Taiya, Paiwan, Bunong, Lukai, Beinan, Cao, Yamei and Saixia. Because the Pingpu people live scattered in Taiwan, they were assimilated with the Hans after the 20th century.

The Gaoshan people are distributed in Taiwan Province over the hills, the eastern flatland and the Lanyu Island ranging from 500 to 2,000 meters above sea level. These tropical and subtropical areas are mostly covered with thick forests.

The Gaoshans mainly grow rice with hunting and fishing as supplement.

The Gaoshan language belongs to the Indonesia group of the Austronesian family. Varying from place to place, the Gaoshan language has 15 branches, which can be classified into 3 groups — the Taiya, Cao and Paiwan. Among them there is no common written form. The Gaoshans on the mainland use Chinese.

1
Gaoshan people on the Great Wall.
2
The Gaoshan people on the mainland and those from Taiwan having a friendly talk.
3
Sharing a bowl of wine side by side is a Gaoshan Tradition. The double-bowl in one piece of wood is unique.
4
Yamei Gaoshans are noted for their exciting Hair Swing Dance, in which dancers are all energetic young women. The dance begins with slow and low songs. As the sound turns louder and the rhythm grows faster, dancers swing their beautiful long hair forward and backward more and more dramatically.
5
A Gaoshan women living in Fujian and her beautiful dress.

2

3

4

THE LAHUS

With a population of 411,476, the Lahus live in close communities in Simao, Lincang in the Lanchang River Valley, Xishuangbanna Dai Autonomous Prefecture, and Honghe Hani-Yi Autonomous Prefecture.

The Lahus make their home in a subtropical mountain area. The climate is cool in summer and warm in winter. In the Lanchang area, rivers meander in high mountains, which are productive and picturesque land rich in various resources.

With two major branches — the Lahuna and Lahuxi, the Lahus are descendants of the ancient Di and Qiang peoples and have close ties with the Yis. In the historical documents of the Qing Dynasty, the Lahus were called "Luohei", but they call themselves "Lahu" meaning "roast tiger". The name shows that the Lahus used to be a hunting tribe. The Kucong people is another branch of the Lahus. After the founding of new China, they were formally called the Lahu Nationality.

The Lahu language belongs to the Yi branch of the Tibeto-Burman group of the Sino-Tibetan family. Many Lahus can speak both Chinese and the Dai language. The written form of the Lahu language was created by a western missionary. Later, on the basis of this system, a Romanization writing became prevalent.

The Lahus are excellent improvisators. Their music uses reed pipes and three-stringed plucked instruments. With repeat stamping and swaying to the left, Lahu dances are dramatic and colorful. For example, the traditional reed pipe dance has about 30 to 40 styles. The Lahus love to make *Tuopuke* (a riddle in the form of poetry). Celebrating the Torch festival is traditional.

1
Celebrating the Lahu New Year.
2
A Lahu dance to worship god.
3
Embroidering a jacket.
4
Keeping water in bottle gourds.

THE DONGXIANGS

The Dongxiang Nationality has a population of 373,872, most in the Dongxiang Autonomous County of Linxia Hui Autonomous Prefecture, Gansu Province. The rest live scattered in Qinghai Province, Ningxia Hui Autonomous Region and Xinjiang Uygur Autonomous Region.

In history, the Dongxiangs were called "Dongxiang Huihui", "Dongxiang Mongols" or "Dongxiang Aborigines", which referred in general to the Moslems living in the Central Asian areas. After the founding of new China, they were generally called the Dongxiang Nationality.

The Dongxiang language resembles to the Mongolian and belongs to the Mongolian group of the Altaic family. It has no written form. Hence, many Dongxiang people have a good command of Chinese.

Located between the Yaohe and Daxia rivers and in the south of the Yellow River, the Dongxiang area is lined by mountains and gullies. Potatoes from Dongxiang are sweet and contain high granulose. Other famous products are watermelon, pears and apricots.

The Dongxiangs have much the same customs, habits and faiths as the Huis in the northwest of China. Everybody loves to sing folk Hua'er songs to express love, freedom and happiness. Among the Dongxiangs, there are many epics and tales. The longest and the most famous are *Meilagahei & Ma Chenglong* and the Tale *the White Wings*. Autumn is the festival season of the villagers. They celebrate their good harvest with art performances and competitions.

1
The traditional dress of Dongxiang women.
2
Dongxiang men greet each other by shaking hands.
3
Living in a cold climate, Dongxiang people love to wear clothes and earmuffs made of fur in winter.
4
Dongxiang potatoes are sweet and contain high granulose.

THE SHUIS

The Shui population is 345,993. Most of them live in Sandu Shui Autonomous County of Qiannan Buyi-Miao Autonomous Prefecture, Libo, Duyun, Dushan, and Kaili, Liping, Rongjiang, Congjiang counties of Qiandongnan Miao-Dong Autonomous Prefecture. A few are scattered in the Guangxi Zhuang Autonomous Region.

The Shuis make their homes in the south of Miaoling mountains, southeast of the Yunnan-Guizhou Plateau and the upper reaches of the Duliu and Longjiang rivers. The picturesque land, covered with lush forests, is arable for farming and forestry and has been developed into a granary and fish pond of Guizhou Plateau.

The Shius plough hard in paddy year after year. Their best wine is called "Jiuqiansa".

Ancestors of the Shuis made up a branch of the ancient Baiyue people. In the Tang and Song dynasties, they were generally called the Liaos together with the Zhuang and Dong peoples. In the Northern Song period, Fushui Prefecture was set up in the Shui area. The name Shui for the first time appeared in the historical documents of the Ming Dynasty. In the Qing Dynasty they were known as "Shuijiamiao" or "Shuijia". After the founding of new China, they were officially called the Shui Nationality.

The Shui language belongs to the Dong-Shui branch of the Zhuang-Dong group of the Sino-Tibetan family. Ancestors of the Shuis created a writing system similar to the oracle-bone and bronze scripts of the ancient Hans. However, it only contains more than 400 characters and merely used by wizards. The Shuis have its own calendar, which resembles the lunar calendar. But a Shui year ends in the eighth month of the lunar calendar, and begins in the ninth. From the end of the eighth to the tenth months, there are four "Hai" days, which are celebrated by different villages alternately. Celebrating the new year's day is called "Jieduan". During this grand festival, young people play reedpipes and beat bronze drums throughout the night. There are horse races, dancing and singing too.

1
A Shui woman wearing elaborate ornaments on her chest.
2
Shui women Embroider beautiful straps for carrying baby.
3
A horse racing competition during the Shuis' *Duan* Festival.

2

5

4
Sharing a bowl of liquor to celebrate the *Duan* Festival.
5
A bronze drum is often used during festivals and ceremonies.

THE NAXIS

The population of the Naxi nationality is 278,009. Most of the Naxi people live in Lijiang Naxi Autonomous County of Yunnan Province in close communities. The rest are scattered in Weixi, Zhongdian, Deqin, Ninglang, and Yongsheng counties.

In ancient times, the nomadic Qiang people, pasturing their cattle in the Yellow and Huangshui river valleys, moved southward to today's southwest Sichuan and northwest Yunnan and separated into several groups. One of them became ancestors of the Naxi people. In the Chinese historical documents, they were called "Mosha", "Moxie", or "Mosuo". In the Naxi language, "Na" means "respectable", while "Xi" means "people". After the founding of new China, they were generally called the Naxi Nationality.

The Naxi language belongs to the Yi branch of the Tibeto-Burman group of the Sino-Tibetan family. Since the Yuan and Ming dynasties, standard Chinese has been adopted, as the Naxis came into closer contact with the Han people. The ancient hieroglyphs, created by Naxi ancestors, were only used by their *Dongba*, the wizard, so it was called the *Dongba* language. The Naxis also have a syllabic script called *Geba*. As the language was only used in a limited area, only a few books written in *Geba* are left.

Located in the south of the Qinghai-Tibet Plateau, the Naxi area is mountainous with big rivers cutting through. The average altitude is 2,700 meters. In the southeast of Zhongdian is the Baha Snow Mountain and in the north of Lijiang is the snowcapped Yulong Mountain, which is noted as a depository of plants. There are more than 40 kinds of azaleas in this area. Rushing from north to south, the swift currents of the Jinsha River are stopped by huge mountains at Shigu Town, forming the first turn on the Changjiang River. As the water moves northeast impetuously, the Yulong and Haba mountains block the river, producing the world famous Tiger-leaping Gorge, which attracts more and more brave explorers each year.

The climate in the Naxi area varies from cold to temperate and subtropical and makes it suitable for farming, forestry and pasture. The rare snow tea and the sturdy Lijiang horses are the world famous products.

1
Naxi women, livining in Muli Eya Township, Sichuan Province, making hemp thread.
2
A wedding ceremony of the Naxis living in Eya.
3
The Mosuos, a branch of the Naxi Nationality, show great respect to the old people especially old women. On festivals, family members can enjoy their meal only after a toast to the oldest woman.
4
When a Mosuo girl is 12 years old, a rite to approve her adulthood is held in her maternal family. Standing on pig fat and a bag of grain, which indicate an ample life in the future, the girl is dressed by the most respectful woman of the family. After the rite, the girl is qualified to take part any tribal activities.
5
It is said that the *Dongba* paintings on wooden slices have the magic power to bring natural pixies under their behest.

6

Naxi women living in Weixi area and their ethnic dress.

THE JINGPOS

The Jingpo population is 119,209. Most of them live in Luxi, Longchuan, Yingjiang, Ruili and Lianghe counties of Dehong Dai-Jingpo Autonomous Prefecture, Yunnan Province.

The Jingpos make their homes in deep mountain areas about 1,500 to 2,000 meters above sea level. The mild climate, adequate rainfall and fertile land enable the plants to grow all the year round. Besides rice, maize and millet, the Jingpo area is rich in mineral resources and produces many valuable cash crops and tropical fruits such as padauk, nanmu, bamboo, rubber, tung tree, coffee, tea, lemongrass, pineapple, jackfruit, mango and bajiao banana. The deep forests are homes of many rare animals and birds.

The Jingpos have close relations with the ancient Di and Qiang peoples coming from the Qinghai-Tibet Plateau. The ancestors of the Jingpos were called "Xunchuanman" or the Gaoligong people in the Tang historical documents. In the Yuan, Ming and Qing dynasties, other names such as "Echang", "Zhexie" and "Yeren" appeared successively. After the founding of new China, they were officially called the Jingpo Nationality.

The Jingpos have five branches. Its language belongs to the Tibeto-Burman group in the Sino-Tibetan family. In the past, they have no written language. At the end of the 20th century, a Romanization writing was created.

1
The grand *Munao* Festival.
2
Jingpo women love to wear straight skirts, which are woven in this way.
3
At a Jingpo wedding, the new couple will step across such a bridge covered with the Chinese character "Xi", meaning happiness.
4
The elephant drum players on the *Munao* Festival.
5
Jingpo men wearing white turbans with colorful small woollen balls decorated on one side. They are called hero knots.

2

3

4

THE KIRGIZES

1
An alpine pasture.
2
The unique clothing of Kirgize women.
3
Embroidering.
4
Wrestling on horseback.

The Kirgizes, with a population of 141,549, live mostly in the Kizilsu Kirgiz Autonomous Prefecture in the southwest of Xinjiang Uygur Autonomous Region and Tekes, Zhaosu and Emin counties in the north.

With the Pamir Plateau and the Tianshan Mountains in the west, oases on the edge of the Tarim Basin in the southeast and the Kizilsu, Gaizi and Kokshar rivers meandering through from the west to east, the Kirgiz area has good pasturelands on the mountain and by the rivers. In the river valleys, an irrigated farming system is developed. On this fertile land, the nomadic Kirgizes tend their cattle year after year supplemented by farming.

In the Han Dynasty, forefathers of the Kirgizes were called "Jiankun" or "Gekun". In the Northern and Southern dynasties, they were refered to as the Jiegus or Qigus, the Jigas in the Tang Dynasty, the Heqis in the Liao and Jin dynasties, the Jilijis in the Yuan Dynasty, and the Bulute people meaning "mountaineers" in Mongolian Juggar language in the Qing Dynasty. After the founding of new China, they were officially called the Kirgiz Nationality.

The Kirgiz language, comprising the northern and southern dialects, belongs to the Turkic group in the Altaic family. When the Kirgizes converted to Islam, they started to use an alphabetic writing based on Arabic letters. Today, as the Kirgizes come into closer contact with other peoples, many of them can speak both the Uighur and Kazak languages.

The Kirgizes have created distinctive literature and arts. *Manass,* a famous epic story in 200,000 lines, portrays the Kirgizes' struggle for freedom. It is a precious literary legacy as well as a treasury of music. The Kirgizes use a special three-stringed plucked musical instrument called "Kaomuzi", which produces rich and harmonious sounds. Kirgiz handicraftsmen make exquisite embroidery, carving, brocade, gold and silver vessels. The Kirgizes celebrate their traditional festivals with various sprightly activities.

THE TUS

With a population of 191,624, the Tu people mostly live in the Huzhu Tu Autonomous County, Minle and Datong counties in the east of Qinghai Province. The rest live scattered in Tongren, Dule and Menyuan.

The Tu area is located in the northeast of the Qinghai-Tibet Plateau. The northern mountainous area is covered with thick forests and stretches of pasturelands. With mild climate and meandering rivers, the southern shallow mountain area has fertile farmland and produces high quality fruits and vegetables.

The name of the Tus varies from place to place. They were also called the Mongol, Qagan, Tukun or Tuhujia people. The Tuyuhun people, active in the Northern and Southern dynasties, is said to be the progenitors of the Tus. In the Tang and Song periods, these people were known as the Tuhuns or Tuihuns, and the Tus in the Yuan Dynasty. After the founding of new China, they were generally called the Tu Nationality.

The Tu language, containing the Huzhu, Minhe and Tongren dialects, belongs to the Mongolian language group of the Altaic family. As the Tu language has no written form, some Tu people can speak both Chinese and Tibetan. Throughout their history, they wrote in Chinese and Tibetan.

Lamaist Buddhism is the principal religion among the Tus. In the early years, Tu ancestors herded a large amount of sheep. In the Ming Dynasty, they took up farming supplemented by raising cattle. Today, every Tu family keeps sheep, and they are still expert herdsmen.

The Tu people possesses two epic songs *The Ode to the Sheep* and *Lajenpu & Chiehmenso*. They love singing very much. Their Hua'er songs are beautiful. Nadun, the carnival of the Tus, perhaps lasts the longest time in the world.

1
The typical dress of Tu women.
2
The so called dustpan headdress is traditional among Tu women.
3
Embroidering sleeve decorations.
4
The ancient dress remains in Tu area.

1
A Daur wedding. Here the bridegroom lifts the veil of his bride happily.
2
At a Daur wedding, the groom's parents welcome the bride's relatives by toasting each of them twice at the doorstep.
3
Making dry beef for later use.
4
A Daur woman.

THE DAURS

The Daurs, with a population of 121,357, mainly live in Morin Dawa Daur Autonomous Banner, and Ewemki Autonomous Banner of Inner Mongolia, Qiqihar City of Heilongjiang Province and Tacheng of Xinjiang. The Daurs, as they call themselves, make their homes by the fertile and beautiful Nenjiang River farming, herding animals, fishing as well as hunting.

The Daur language, containing the Butha, Qiqihar and Xinjiang dialects, belongs to the Mongolian language group of the Altaic family. As the Daurs have come into close contact with other peoples for a fairly long time, most Daurs have a good command of Chinese, Mongolian, Uigur, Kazak and Ewenki languages.

In the past years, the name of Daur was translated as "Dahur" or "Dagur". The word "Daur" firstly appeared in the early years of the Ming Dynasty. Historical records show that the Daurs are descendants of the Khitan tribe of the Liao Dynasty because of the common language, customs, habits and geographic distribution.

1

2

3

4

THE MULAMS

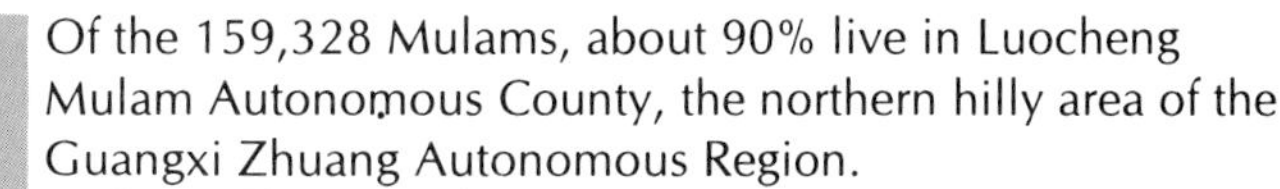

Of the 159,328 Mulams, about 90% live in Luocheng Mulam Autonomous County, the northern hilly area of the Guangxi Zhuang Autonomous Region.

Mulam villages are built in the undulate mountains with ripply rivers meandering about. The land, rich in mineral resources and mountain products, is so attractive that many tourists say it rivals Guilin in natural beauty.

Rice is planted as the staple crop. Coal mining and gathering are also important.

Many Mulams call themselves "Muleng" or "Lingren". In the Jin Dynasty, they were refered to as the Liaos. After the Tang and Song dynasties, they were better known as the Liao or Ling people in historical documents. In the Qing dynasty, these people were called the Mulaos. After the founding of new China, they took the name Mulam.

The Mulam language belongs to the Dong-Shui branch of Zhuang-Dong Group of the Sino-Tibetan family. As the language has no script, many Mulam people use Chinese and the Zhuang language.

The polytheistic Mulams, mainly Daoists and Buddhists, take holidays every month except the tenth and the eleventh. The annual *Yifan* festival is the most important occasion. Every three years, there is a grand celebration for this festival.

1
The picturesque Mulam area attracts more and more tourists each year.
2
A Mulam woman.
3
During festivals, antiphonal singing is a common means of courtship among the Mulam youths.
4
Washing by the river.

THE QIANGS

Of the total 198,252 Qiang people, most live in Maowen County of Aba Tibet-Qiang Autonomous Prefecture in Sichuan Province. Others live scattered in Wenchuan, Lixian, Heishui, Songpan, Tanpa of Kantze Tibet Autonomous Prefecture and Beichuan of Mianyang City.

As an ancient ethnic group, the Qiangs were recorded in the historical documents of the Yin period in the oracle-bone script as early as 3,000 years ago. The Qiang area is located on the east edge of the Qinghai-Tibet Plateau. Surrounded by high mountains, thick forests and swift currents, this gorge area is rich in various resources especially valuable medicinal herbs and rare animals such as giant panda and golden monkey.

The Qiangs grow crops and also raise animals supplemented by hunting and other sideline occupations.

The Qiang language, containing the southern and northern dialects, belongs to the Qiang Branch (or the Tibetan branch) of the Tibeto-Burman group of the Sino-Tibetan family. As the language has no written form, the Qiangs write Chinese. The Dangxiang Qiang, ancestors of the present Qiangs, created the Xixia script in the Xixia Kingdom period. Later it became a dead language, no one could read it until the early years of the 20th century.

2

3

4

5

1
Threshing corn.
2
Sewing wedding clothes.
3
When out for working, Qiang women often wear sleeveless sheepskin jackets as shoulder pads.
4
A Qiang woman.
5
Qiang women.

THE BLANGS

The Blangs, with a population of 82,280, mainly live in close communities in the Blang, Xiding, Bada, and Daluo mountains of Menghai County in Xishangbanna, Yunnan Province. The remainder are scattered in Lincang and Simao. The Blangs are descendants of the ancient Pus. In the Tang Dynasty, they were called "Puziman", and "Puman" in the Yuan, Ming and Qing dynasties. In the past, the appellation of these people differed from place to place. After the founding of new China, they were generally named the Blang Nationality in accordance with their wishes.

The Blangs make their homes in a subtropical mountain area about 1,500 to 2,300 meters above sea level. The rolling mountains are covered with thick primeval forests. For the mild and rainy climate, tung and camphor trees are flourishing. Most Blangs engage in farming, growing dry rice, tea and cotton. Their tea is the raw material for the world famous Pu'er Tea.

The Blang language belongs to the Va-De'ang branch of the Austro-Asiatic family. As the language has no script, Blang people speak the Dai, Va and Chinese languages. Some write Chinese and the Dai language.

1
A Blang wedding ceremony.
2
A Blang woman.
3
Young people enjoy full freedom in love and marriage.
4
Since their farms are far from their houses, Blang people often have lunch in the field.
5
The carrying basket used by Blang women normally has a long belt, which they put on the head when the basket is fully loaded.

THE SALARS

The Salars, with a population of 87,697, mainly live in close community in Xunhua Salar Autonomous County of Qinghai Province. A few are scattered in Qinghai, Gansu and Xinjiang.

Located in the east of Qinghai Province, and by the Yellow River, the Salar area enjoys mild climate and strong and long sunshine time, which is suitable for the growth of crops. The Salars grow wheat, *qingke* barley, buckwheat, maize, millet, fruit and vegetable. Xunhua pepper is a famous local product.

Early in the Yuan Dynasty, the Samarkand people in the Central Asia, who were believed to be the ancestors of the Salars, traveled eastward to Xunhua by way of Xinjiang. Over the years, they, calling themselves "Salar", mixed with the Tibetans, Hans and Huis living in the surrounding area and gradually came to form a new tribe. In the old days, the Hans called them the Sala, Shala, Shalacu, or Sala Hui people. After the founding of new China, they took the name Salar.

The Salar language, enriched with the Han and Tibetan vocabulary owing to the close contact, belongs to the Western Xiong branch of the Turkic group of the Altaic family. As the language has no written form, many Salars write with Chinese.

Influenced by Islam, the Salars, most of whom are Moslems, have much the same customs as the nearby Huis. Men grow beards and wear black or white flat-topped, round caps and black vests over white shirts. Women wear turbans and shining gold and silver earrings and bracelets. The Salars excel in doing business, tanning and chopping trees. Horticulture is well developed. On swift currents of the Yellow River, they are very skillful in steering rafts.

1
Salar young people reaping wheat.
2
Salar women embroidering in their spare time.
3
A well-off Salar family.
4
Killing sheep on the Festival of Fast-breaking.

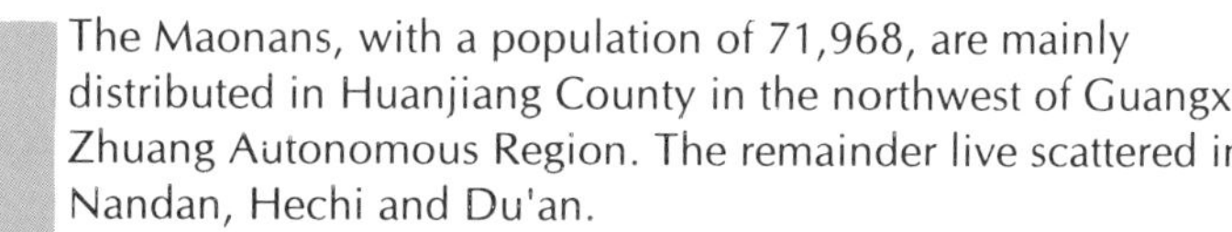

THE MAONANS

1
The Maonan Bamboo Hat Dance.
2
A Maonan woman.
3
During festivals, Maonan young people knead multicolored glutinous rice into small balls and stick them to a bamboo branch. It is said that the decorated branch will bring a good year for the family.
4
Pole wrenching is a traditional sport.

The Maonans, with a population of 71,968, are mainly distributed in Huanjiang County in the northwest of Guangxi Zhuang Autonomous Region. The remainder live scattered in Nandan, Hechi and Du'an.

The Maonan area is located in the eastern foothills of the Yunnan-Guizhou Plateau. The Maonan Mountain stands in the middle with the Jiuwan Dashan Mountain in the northeast, the Fenghuang Mountain in the northwest and the Dashi Mountain region in the southwest. The rolling mountains are covered with thick forests. Deep karst caves can be easily found. Here the subtropical climate is suitable for crops and cattle.

Farming, supplemented by raising animals and sidelines, is the chief occupation of the Maonans. They grow rice and many other crops.

The Maonans call themselves Anan, meaning "local people". It shows that the Maonans are the aborigines of this area. Ancestors of the Maonans had some relations with the Liaos before the Tang Dynasty and the Lings of the Song, Yuan and Ming periods. In history, they were known as "Maotan", "Angtan", and "Maonan" successively.

The Maonan language belongs to the Dong-Shui branch of Zhuang-Dong Group of the Sino-Tibetan family. The language has no written form. In the past, Chinese characters were used to record Maonan folk songs. This method of transliteration was called the Tusu script. At present, Maonan people speak both the Zhuang language and Chinese and write in Chinese.

THE GELOS

1
A beautiful Gelo village.
2
Picking Chinese galls.
3
Gelo people playing folk musical instruments in their spare time.
4
A Gelo woman embroidering.

The Gelos, with a population of 437,997, live in Wuchuan Gelo Autonomous County and Daozhen Gelo-Miao Autonomous County of Guizhou Province. A small number are scattered in Yunnan and Guangxi.

Located in the north of Guizhou Province and bordering on Sichuan Province, the Gelo area is in a large transitional region between the Sichuan Basin and the Yunnan-Guizhou Plateau. With complicate landforms and excess rainfall, this area reserves rich water, plant and animal resources and is suitable for agriculture and a diverse economy.

Farming is the chief occupation of the Gelo people. On flatland they plant rice, while in mountainous areas, they grow other crops, thus developing a kind of rice-growing economy.

The Gelo people possess an extremely long history. Their ancestors have close relations with the Baipus of the Shang, Zhou and the Western Han periods, and the Pus and Liaos of the Eastern Han, and the Southern and Northern dynasties. Later, historical records referred to them as the Geliao, or Gelo people. After the founding of new China, they were officially called the Gelo Nationality.

The Gelo language is under the Sino-Tibetan language family. However, as to which branch and group does the language belong to, linguists consider variously. Now, only a few old Gelo people can speak their native language. As the Gelo language has no script, Chinese is now their common language.

1
A Xibo woman.
2
Beilen is a traditional Xibo dance.
3
Making bows and arrows.
4
Many ancient customs remain among the Xibos. For example, old Xibo people greet each other with bows.

THE XIBES

The Xibes, with a population of 83,629, mainly live in Liaoning, Jilin provinces, and Qapqal Xibe Autonomous County of Ili Prefecture, Xinjiang.

The Xibe people believe themselves to be descended from the Sienpis, who were initially herdsmen hunting and fishing in the eastern foothills of the Greater Hinggan Mountains. In the 16th century, after these people were brought under the Eight-Banner system, their social organization changed dramatically as farming became the chief occupation. In the mid-18th century, the Qing government had some Xibes transferred to the south bank of the Ili River to strengthen the garrison forces in Xinjiang, and that split the Xibes into two major groups.

With the continuous efforts of the diligent Xibes, the Qapqal Cannel running more than 100 kilometers was built on the deserted land. The valuable water turned the former barren desert into productive farms and beautiful orchards.

The Xibes are noted for their valiant spirit, equestrian and archery skills. Today, some Xibes emerge as excellent archers. The Xibe language belongs to the Manchu-Tungusic group of the Altaic family. They have long absorbed the cultural creams of other nationalities by way of serious translation. Even several hundred years ago, the Xibo version of the famous novels such as *the Romance of Three Kingdoms* and *Pilgrims to the West* were very popular.

Though some Xibes are Shamanists and some are Lamaists, they both offer sacrifices to their ancestors. The 18th day of the fourth month in the Lunar Year is the commemoration day of the Xibes in Xinjiang, marking the arrival at this northwest border after a long journey from the east.

1

2

4

THE ACHANGS

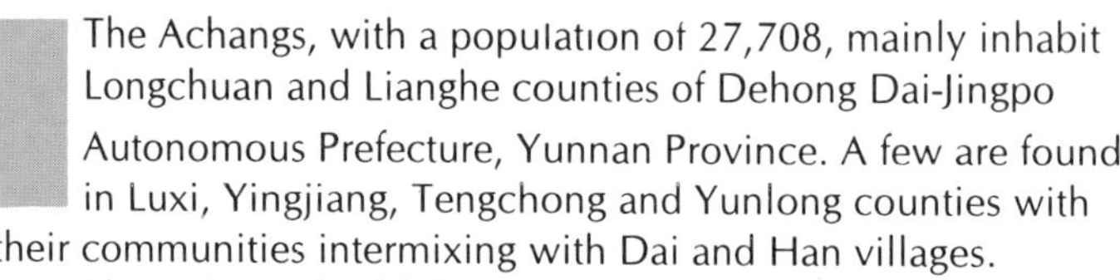

The Achangs, with a population of 27,708, mainly inhabit Longchuan and Lianghe counties of Dehong Dai-Jingpo Autonomous Prefecture, Yunnan Province. A few are found in Luxi, Yingjiang, Tengchong and Yunlong counties with their communities intermixing with Dai and Han villages.

The Achangs build their homes in the Gaoligong Mountains farming on tiny plains, and in river valleys. The land is fertile and the water abundant, suitable for fine rice strains, which the Achangs are noted for.

As the aborigines in the territory of Yunnan, historical records of different periods referred to these people as the Echangs or Achangs. After the founding of New China, they were generally called the Achang Nationality.

The Achang language, containing the Lianghe and Husa dialects, belongs to the Tibeto-Burman group of the Sino-Tibetan family. As the Achangs have long amalgamated with the Hans and Dais, most Achang people can speak both Chinese and the Dai language.

1
An Achang wedding ceremony. When the groom meets his bride, her sisters will play tricks on him. First, they blacken the groom's face with ashes and then force the groom to pick up a piece of meat with their deliberately prepared bamboo sticks, which are much more longer than the normal chopsticks. As there are several tricksy relatives, the groom's simple task seems extremely hard to accomplish. What a poor groom and what an amusing wedding ceremony!

2
An Achang family normally has three cauldrons on one kitchen range. The unique design makes it quite convenient for cooking.

3
Achang women living in Lianghe Prefecture love to wear black turbans.

4
An Achang young man performing with a sword.

5
Various Achang knives and swords.

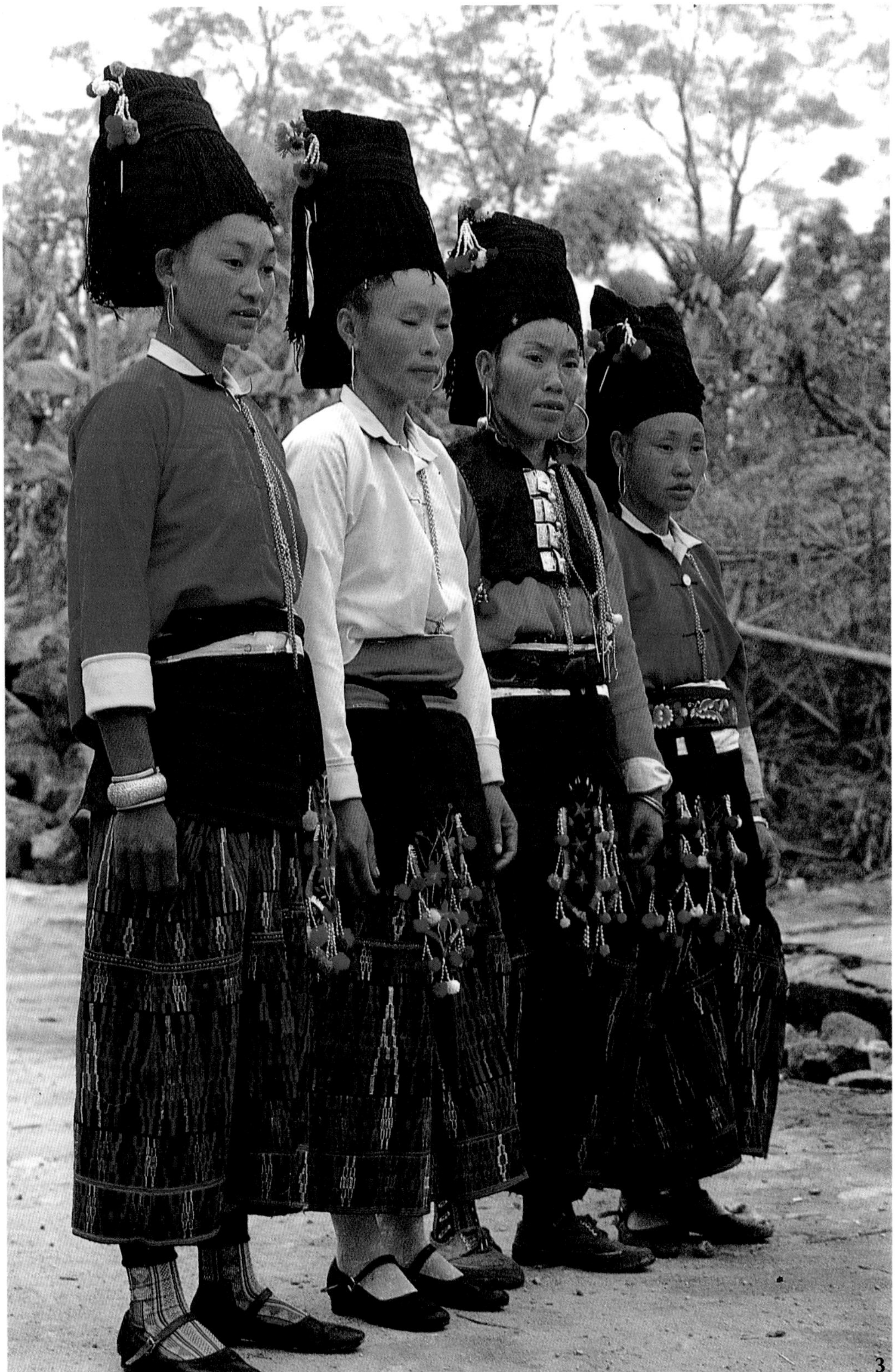

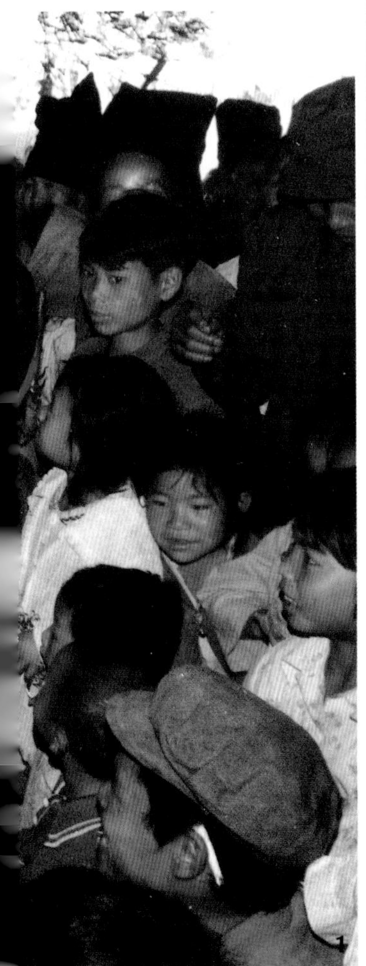

6
An Achang woman living in Husa.

THE PRIMIS

The Primis, with a population of 29,657, mainly live in the Laojun Mountain of Lanping and the foothills of the Maoniu Mountain of Ninglang in the northwest of Yunnan Province. A small number can be found in Lijiang, Yongsheng, Weixi, Zhongdian, and Yanyuan, Muli of Sichuan Province living side by side with other ethnic groups.

The Primis call themselves "Puyingmi", "Purimi" or "Peimi", meaning "white people". Historical records referred to them as the Xifans or the Bajus. After the founding of new China, they were officially called the Primi Nationality with their approval.

The Primi language belongs to the Qiang branch of the Tibeto-Burman group of the Sino-Tibetan family. Dialect variations are usually slight. Many Primis speak the Chinese, Tibetan, Bai and Naxi languages. In history, the Primis living in Ninglang and Muli used the Tibetan script to transliterate their legends, tales, and songs. However, this written form was only adopt by sorcerers to compose scriptures. At present, Chinese has become widespread among the Primis.

The Primi religion combines animism with deep respect for ancestors. A few are Taoists and Lamaist Buddhists. The primary festivals of the Primis are the Spring Festival, Dashiwu (on the 14th day of the last month in the lunar year), and the *Changxin* Festival.

1
The Primi people living in Ninglang area celebrate their annual *Changxin* Festival.
2
Though dress of the Primis living in Laojun Mountains of Lanping resembles that of the neighboring Bais, there is a distinct diversity of customs between the two. Here a Primi woman is going to show her vocal imitation skills with a piece of tender rattan.
3
A Primi old woman is weaving.
4
Coming back from a fair.

1
Celebrating the Tajik Lantern Festival.
2
Tajik women greet each other by kisses.
3
Washing.
4
A horse racing competition.

THE TAJIKS

The Tajiks, with a population of 33,538, mainly live in Taxkorgan Tajik Autonomous County in the southwest of Xinjiang Uygur Autonomous Region. A few can be found in Shache, Zepu, Yecheng and Pishan counties in the western edge of the Tarim Basin.

Located in the eastern part of the Pamir Plateau, Taxkorgan is surrounded by many high mountains. In the south is the world second highest peak — the Qogir rising 8,611 meters above sea level. In the north is the snowcapped Muztagata mountain at an altitude of 7,546 meters, which brings forth a large amount of huge and amazing glaciers at its foot. The flatland in the river valleys of these mountains has been built into productive farms by the enterprising Tajiks.

As early as the pre-Qin period, ancestors of the Tajiks had made their homes on the Pamirs. From the 2nd century B.C., Taxkorgan had become an important passage when the Silk Road was opened. Throughout their history, the Tajiks actively absorbed the creams of both eastern and western cultures and developed a distinctive history and civilization of their own.

The Tajik people, most of them are Moslems, have their own language, but the commonly used is the Uygur language. Their nomad life is supplemented by farming.

The Tajiks are by nature straightforward and strong. In their ancient legends, an eagle symbolizes heroism. They make flutes out of eagle bones and imitate the eagle's movements in dance. Moreover, the Tajiks are excellent riders who frequently hold contests in horsemanship such as polo and sheep snatching.

THE NUS

With a population of 27,123, the Nus, calling themselves "Nusu", "Anu" or "Along", mainly live in Lushui, Fugong, Gongshan and Lanping counties of Nujiang Lisu Autonomous Prefecture, Weixi county of Deqen Tibet Autonomous Prefecture of Yunnan Province and Zayu County of Tibet side by side with the Lisu, Drung, Tibetan, Bai, Han and Naxi people.

The Nu language, having no written form, belongs to the Tibeto-Burman group of the Sino-Tibetan family with such a distinct diversity of local dialects, that different tribes among the Nus can hardly communicate with each other. But, the Lisu language is common among the Nus, because they have lived for centuries near the Lisu people.

The Nu Nationality is one of the oldest ethnic groups in the Nujiang and Lancang River area. Rapid rivers, jagged mountains, high peaks, roaring waterfalls and lush trees and bamboo together form the great natural beauty of this area, which is quite favorable for tourism. However, this beautiful land, cut off by mountains and rivers, is poor and quite difficult for access. Social progress among the Nus was deterred. Before the founding of new China, their society remained at the primitive stage. Slash-and-burn farming was prevalent. They simply recognize seasons by flowers, keep track of time and send massage by typing knots in rope and making notches on wood. Though the living conditions are difficult, the Nus are by nature diligent and brave. Their unceasing struggle with nature will surely bring this beautiful land a bright future.

1
The great natural beauty of the Nujiang River Valley is really admirable. There are several waterfalls like this one in the valley.
2
Bows and arrows accompany a man throughout his life.
3
Pulling up rice seedlings for transplanting.
4
The Nu women's straight skirt is woven in this way.
5
Canoes have been used by the Nus for generations.

3

2

4

THE UZBEKS

The Uzbeks, with a population of 12,453, live mostly side by side with the Uygur and Kazak peoples in the southern and northern parts of Xinjiang Uygur Autonomous Region. The Uzbeks derived from the Uzbek kingdom of the Mongolian Kipchak Khanate in the 14th century. When the Kipchak Khanate collapsed in the 15th century, Uzbek businessmen living in Samarkand, Khwarizm, Anjiyan and Bukhara came to sell their goods in the Central Plains of China along the Silk Road by way of Xinjiang. Later, some of these businessmen settled down in several towns of Xinjiang and formed the Uzbek people of China.

Today, most Uzbek people live in towns and have become government workers or craftsmen. A small number living in the north raise animals while few farm in the south. For centuries, the Uzbeks have had close contacts with other nationalities living in Xinjiang, especially with the Uygurs and Kazaks. Their languages, customs, and faiths influenced each other and became similar in many details.

The Uzbek language, using Arabic alphabet, belongs to the Western Xiong branch of the Turkic group of the Altaic family. Most Uzbek people can speak both the Uygur and Kazak languages.

The Uzbeks are Moslems. Their dance movements are graceful, brisk and twirling. Among the many musical instruments, the most popular are plucked and percussion instruments. Uzbek women are good at embroidery. Exquisite patterns can be easily founded on their clothes, hats, sheet and pillows.

1
It's happy to hear from the outside world.
2
Uzbek women excel in embroidery. Gorgeous tapestries are some of the most characteristic Uzbek handicrafts.
3
Uzbek women love to wear colorful shawls.
4
Daddy bought me a new toy.

1
A beautiful Russian woman.
2
Chatting.
3
The accordion is a favorite musical instrument of the Russians. During festivals, people usually play it, while others dance happily.
4
Russian old people select garlic.

THE RUSSIANS

The Russians, with a population of 13,504, mainly live in Ili, Tacheng, Altay and Urumqi of Xinjiang Autonomous Region. The rest are scattered in the Inner Mongolia Autonmous Region and Heilongjiang Province.

First migrating here in the 18th century, the Russian ethnics have lived in China for nearly 200 years. Immigration in the early years of the 19th century brought many more to Xinjiang. At that time, they were called the Guihua people, while their communities were called Guihua villages. After the founding of new China, they were formally called the Russian Nationality. Though small in number, the Russians share equal political rights with other peoples. Their living conditions were also improved rapidly in the past decades.

The Russian language belongs to the Slavonic group of the Indo-European family. In social activities, Russian people use Chinese, but in their families or contacting with natives, they use the Russian language.

Russian clothing is rich and colorful. Men wear uniform, breeches, boots or leather shoes. Women wear dresses. The middle-aged persons are mostly in the Han dress or in western suits, but young people prefer fashionable clothes.

The Russians are Eastern Orthodox Christians.

Most Russians live in urban area and work as technicians and skilled workers and some well-educated in cultural and educational enterprises. Russian farmers fish, grow fruit and keep bees.

THE EWENKIS

The Ewenkis, with a population of 26,315, mainly live in Ewenki Autonomous Banner of Hulun Buir Meng, Inner Mongolian Autonomous Region. Others can be found in the Chen Barag Banner, Ergun Left Banner, Morin Dawa Banner, Arun Banner, Zhalantun City, and Nehe County of Heilongjiang Province with their communities intermixing with local Mongolian, Daur, Han and Oroqen people.

Situated in the hills of the Greater Hinggan Mountains, the Ewenki area is covered with thick virgin forests and stretches of grasslands, with a network of big and small rivers meandering through. Differing natural conditions have created differing lifestyles. In the Ewenki Autonomous County and Chen Barag Banner, people mainly breed animals. Those in Nehe county are farmers. In Morin Dawa Banner, Arun Banner, Zhalantun City, the Ewenki people till the earth as well as hunt. Those in the Ergun Left Banner hunt with reindeer, hence their nickname "the Ewenkis who use reindeer".

In the past, different settlements of the migratory Ewenkis had been called by different names such as "Suolun", "Tungus" and "Yakute". But in 1957, they took the name Ewenki meaning "people living deep in the mountains and forests".

The Ewenkis are Shamanists and those living in the pastoral area are Lamaist Buddhists. The Ewenki language, containing the Hui-Yimin, Mergel and Alruguya dialects, belongs to the Manchu-Tungusic group of the Altaic language family. Herdsmen in the pastoral region speak the Mongolian language, and those in the farming and mountain areas use Chinese.

1
In spring and autumn, Ewenki people often have their meals in the open.
2
A newly married couple in a reindeer farm.
3
When spring comes, the Ewenkis usually organize art performances and competitions, which attract many neighboring residents.
4
An Ewenki woman.

THE BONANS

The Bonans, with a population of 12,212, mostly live in close communities in Jishishan Bonan-Dongxiang-Sala Autonomous County of Gansu Province. A few can be found in Linxia Hui Autonomous Prefecture of Gansu and Xunhua County of Qinghai Province.

Located in the southwest of Gansu Province, the Bonan area borders on Linxia county in the southeast and Xunhua Salar Autonomous County of Qinghai in the west. The Yellow River separates this area from Minhe County of Qinghai and Yongjing County of Gansu in the north and northeast. At the foot of Jishi Mountain and on the upper reaches of the Yellow River, the fertile land is suitable for farming and raising animals. Wheat, maize, potato, *qingke* barley. and pea are the staple crops. Their juicy pear and thin cover walnut are popular products.

In history, the Bonan people were called "Huihui" or "Bonan Hui". After the founding of new China, they took the name Bonan Nationality.

The Bonan language, without a script, belongs to the Mongolian group in the Altaic family. Most Bonans speak Chinese.

The Bonans are Moslems. Their family and social life, customs and habits closely resemble those of the neighboring Hui and Dongxiang minorities.

The Bonans engage in farming and herding as well as handicraft. In a fairly early time, the Bonans knew how to smelt iron and possessed high skills of making knives. Their sharp, durable and exquisite hunting knives, praised as Bonan Knives, are popular among local people.

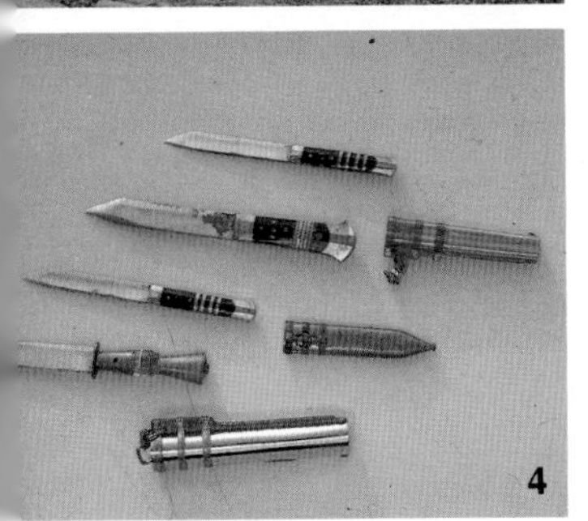

1
Walking tractors help Bonan people to get rich.
2
The Bonan women's headdresses.
3
The Bonans living in the upper reaches of the Yellow River use these sheepskin rafts to cross the river.
4
Bonan knives.

THE DE'ANGS

The De'angs, with a population of 15,462, live scattered in Luxi County of Dehong Dai-Jingpo Autonomous Prefecture, and Zhenkang County of Lincang Prefecture in Yunnan Province. Some can be found in Yingjiang, Ruili, Longchuan, Baoshan,Lianghe, Longling and Gengma counties intermixing with the Jingpos, Hans, Lisus, Vas and Dais.

As one of the oldest tribes in the southwest border area, the De'angs, derived from the ancient Pu people, are descendants of the Mangman Tribe. After the founding of new China, they used to be called the Benglong Nationality. Later in 1985, they took the named De'ang.

The De'angs live in loose communities, often side by side with the Hans, Dais, Jingpos and Vas. Hence their religion, habits and customs have long been influenced by the above mentioned peoples, especially the Dais.

The De'angs love sour and hot food and strong tea. Known as the Ancient Tea Growers, the De'angs excel in gathering wild plants and growing tea, and every family possesses tea trees of fine strains. They are also good weavers of bamboo wares and thatched roofs. Their traditional silver vessels enjoy high fame among the neighboring peoples.

The De'ang language, with three dialects, belongs to the Va-Ang branch of the Austro-Asiatic family. Many De'angs speak Chinese, the Dai and Jingpo languages.

1
Driving cattle home.
2
A De'ang woman.
3
Weaving a straight skirt.
4
A festival meal on the balcony of a De'ang bamboo cottage.
5
Respecting the elderly is a tradition of the De'ang people. During festivals, younger people usually send gifts to the old.

2

3

1
The Qilian Mountains in autumn.
2
Yugur herdsmen.
3
Yugur women, living in the east of the Qilian Mountains, wear richer dress. Elaborate embroideries can be found on their collars, chests and sleeves. They also wear colorful necklaces.
4
Yugur women use self-made knitting wool to weave winter aprons.
5
Teachers give regular lessons to children living in remote pastures.

THE YUGURS

The Yugurs, with a population of 10,569, mainly live in Sunan Yugur Autonomous County and Huangnibao Yugur Township of Jiuquan City, Gansu Province.

The Yugurs are descended from an ethnic group known in the Tang Dynasty as Huigu, who roamed in the Ergun River Basin. In the mid-9th century, a branch of the Huigu group settled down in today's Dunhuang, Zhangye and Wuwei in the Hexi Corridor of Gansu Province. Therefore, they were called "Hexi Huigu" in history. Later, the close contacts between these people and neighboring minorities, helped the formation of a new nationality.

The Yugurs call themselves "Yaohu'er". According to historical records, ancestors of the Yugurs were called "Huangtou Huigu" in the Song Dynasty, "Sali Weiwu" in the Yuan Dynasty, "Sali Weiwuerh" in the Ming Dynasty and "Xila Weiguerh" in the Qing Dynasty. After the founding of new China, they were generally called the Yugur Nationality with their wishes.

Located in the middle part of the Hexi Corridor, which is a narrow zone in the northern foothills of the Qilian Mountains, the Yugur areas are excellent natural pastures covered with thick virgin forests and home of a great number of rare wild animals and plants. The Qilian Mountains reserve rich mineral resources, and the valuable jadestone makes the Yugur people world famous.

The Yugurs use three languages. The western Yugurs living in the west of Sunan Yugur Autonomous County speak the Yaohu'er language, which belongs to the Turkic group of the Altaic family. The Eastern Yugur language or called Enger, used by those living in the east of Sunan Yugur Autonomous County, belongs to the Mongolian group of the Altaic family. Chinese is mainly used in Huangnibao of Jiuquan and Shuanghai area of Sunan. As the Yugur languages have no script, Chinese is the common communicating and writing language among the different groups of the Yugurs.

The Yugurs, most of them are herdsmen, believe in Lamaism. Their customs and habits are similar to the Tibetans.

2

3

1

4

5

THE JINGS

The Jings, with a population of 18,915, live in Wanwei, Shanxin, Wutou and Tanji villages of Fangcheng City, Guangxi Zhuang Autonomous Region.

These subtropical islands produce a large amount of sea products. In addition to the more than 700 kinds of fish, the pearl, sea horse and sea otter are the most famous.

The Jings are good fishermen as well as farmers. They developed an economy combining coastal fishery and farming.

The Jings' ancestors formerly lived in Jipo of Vietnam. About 400 years ago, some, living in the coastal area Tushan, migrated and settled down in the Wutou Island. In history, the Jings were called "Yuezu". After the founding of new China, they were officially called the Jing Nationality.

The Jings are Catholics or Taoists. They have their language, but they speak and write Chinese.

1
Every Jing woman is a hand both at home and work.
2
***Du Xian Qin*, a traditional musical instrument, has only a single string and a body made of half a bamboo tube.**
3
Pulling the net.
4
A Jing family.
5
Going to sea.

3

5

THE TARTARS

The Tartars, with a population of 4,127, mainly live in Yining, Tacheng, Altay, and Urumqi of Xinjiang Uygur Autonomous Region. A few are distributed in Burqin and Qitai.

In history, the Tartars were called "Dadan", "Tartar" or "Dada". In the mid-15th century, Tartar people established the Kashan Khanate in the area between the Volga River and the Kama River. In the early years of the 20th century, some Kashan people migrated to Xinjiang and later made up a minority group of China.

The Tartar language belongs to the Western Xiong branch of the Turkic group of the Altaic family. Its written form is based on the Arabic letters. As the Tartars have long intermixed with the Uygurs and Kazaks, they gradually adopted their languages.

In history, the Tartars living in cities are good businessmen and some worked in educational enterprises. In the past century, they have made great contribution to the construction of Xinjiang. Today, as the market economy develops, the traditional mercantile people is playing an increasingly important role in society.

The Tartars are Moslems. Their baked cake and pastry are very popular in Xinjiang.

1
Tartar musicians.
2
As the Tartars have long mixed with the Kazaks and Uygurs, their cultures show many resemblances. Though Tartar clothing has changed quite a lot, nomadic traces still remain.
3
Tartar children.
4
The modern dress of Tartar women.

THE OROQENS

The Oroqens, with a population of 6,965, mainly live in Oroqen Autonomous Banner, Morin Dawa Banner, Arun Banner, Zhalantun City of Inner Mongolia Autonomous Region and Tahe, Huma, Xunke, Jiayin counties and Heihe City of Heilongjiang Province.

The Oroqens make their homes in the Greater and Lesser Hinggan Mountains, which form the backbone of the Northeast China and the Heilongjiang River Basin. The Greater Hinggan Mountains, with towering peaks, deep valleys and meandering streams, extend from the northeast to the southwest in Heilongjiang Province and Inner Mongolia Autonomous Region. The Lesser Hinggan Mountains stretch gently from the upper reaches of the Heilong River to the southeast. The mountains, covered with primeval forests, yield many medical herbs and hardy trees such as larch, Korean pine, birch, oak and poplar. The special mountain products are Jew's ear, mushroom, hazelnut and persimmon. The thick forests are home of a great number of rare beasts and birds. For generations, the Oroqens roamed and hunted deer in the immense forests all the year round with their guns, horses and hunting dogs untile the 1950s.

The word Oroqen has two meanings. One is "people living high in the mountains"; the other is "people who use reindeer". Before the Qing Dynasty, the Oroqens were called the Suolun, Dasheng or Shilu tribe. After the founding of new China, they were generally called the Oroqen Nationality.

The Shamanist Oroqens worship their ancestors and adore animism. Their language, without a script, belongs to the Tungus branch of the Manchu-Tungusic group of the Altaic language family. Many Oroqens speak the Chinese, Ewenki and Daur languages. They generally write in Chinese.

Various birch bark wares and birch bark cockboats are some of the most characteristic handicrafts of the Oroqens. The exquisite patterns on birch boats are the vivid illustration of their long hunting tradition.

1
Gloves made of wild dog skin.
2
A bag made of roe deer skin.
3
Children wear such deer skin boots.
4
Sledges are the major transport in winter.

5
Cooking in the open.
6
Oroqen women making clothes with roe deer skin.
7
Reindeer raised by Oroqen people.
8
Oroqen children wear hats and coats made of roe deer skin.
9
When an Oroqen mother works in the field, she simply hangs the cradle on a branch.

CHINA'S MINORITY PEOPLES

THE DRUNGS

The Drungs, with a population of 5,817, mainly live in Nujiang Lisu Autonomous Prefecture, and along the banks of the Dulong River in Gongshan Drung-Nu Autonomous County in the northwest Yunnan Province.

In the past, the Drungs have no general appellation. They named themselves by rivers or places such as "Dulong" and "Dima". The Hans called them the Qiu, Qiuzi or Qu people. After the founding of new China, they took the name Drung.

The Drung area borders on Zayu of Tibet in the north and Burma in the southwest. In the east is the 5,000-meter-high Gaoligong Mountain, through which flow the swift currents of the Dulong River. From the bottom of deep valley to the top of high mountains, the climate changes vertically, so do the species of plants. In winter, this river valley is completely cut off by snow, while in summer, it is humid and rainy because of the tropical monsoon from the Indian Ocean.

Drung society had long been primitive owing to the semi-locked location. Slash-and-burn farming was prevalent. Gathering and hunting are important parts of the economy.

The Drung language, without a script, is an independent branch of the Tibeto-Burman group of the Sino-Tibetan family. Some Drungs speak Chinese.

The Drungs by nature are diligent, brave and simple-minded. They keep their promises and have good credit. They never use locks for safety. The barns are simply marked by crossed branches and free from stealing. In addition, the Drungs are hospitable and willing to help others. Once, a family is in difficulty, other villagers offer their generous aids without any hesitation. Today, though the modern life has changed the Drungs quite a lot, their fine traditions remain.

2

4

1
During the Spring Festival, a bull is usually killed by a Drung young man, as others beat gongs and dance with knives and swords.
2
Fishing by the Dulong River.
3
Weaving a Drung carpet.
4
Cooking on a stone stove.
5
In the past, girls at 12 or 13, normally had their faces tattooed. Today, this ancient custom has been out of date.

THE HEZHENS

The Hezhen Nationality, with a population of 4,245, is one of the smallest ethnic groups of China. Most Hezhen people live in close communities in Jiejinkou, Sipai and Bacha townships of Raohe and Fuyuan counties, Heilongjiang Province.

In ancient times, ancestors of the Hezhens live in the Heilong, Songhua and Wusuli river valleys. They were variously called the Heijin, Heizhen, Hezhen, Qileng or Hezhe people in different historical periods. After the founding of new China, these people were generally called the Hezhen Nationality, meaning "people living in the east or the lower reaches of rivers".

The Hezhen language, with a lot of expressions similar to the Manchu language, belongs to the Manchu-Tungusic group of the Altaic family. But now only old people can speak it. As the Hezhen language has no script, they use Chinese.

Traditionally, the Hezhens are Shamanists. They lived in a rich mountain area with many rivers meandering through. The excellent natural environment made the Hezhens excel in hunting and fishing. It was said that the Hezhen area was so rich that the Hezhens could hunt roe deer with stick, fish with bowl and wild ducks were often found on the dining table. At present, fishing is the most important part in the Hezhens' economy and thus forms the basis of the unique but rich native culture. The Hezhens, young and old, men and women, are good fishermen.

1
The Hezhens build their houses with logs.
2
The Hezhens living by the Usuli River love to embroider colorful cloud patterns on their hats and garments.
3
Hezhen women mending a fishing net.
4
Sharing fresh fish meat.
5
Today, living conditions in the Hezhen area have been improved. When a guest comes, the Hezhen family usually cook fish for him.

THE MOINBAS

The Moinbas, with a population of 7,475, mainly live in Medog and Cona Counties of Tibet. A few inhabit Zayu and Nyingchi counties.

In the southeast of the Himalaya Range, the Yarlung Zangbo River makes a sharp turn to the south at Medog and Nyingchi, cutting deep valleys. According to Tibetan historical records, ancestors of the Moinbas made their homes in this gorge area more than a thousand years ago. Fortunately, the Moinba area has a mild climate, adequate rainfall, fertile soil and rich produce. However, owing to lack of easy transport, very few outsiders have the chance to visit this beautiful land.

In the 13th century, the Moinyu area in the south of Cona was brought to the domain of the Chinese government as a part of Tibet. Over a long period of time, the Moinbas forged close economic, political, cultural and religious ties with Tibet. They use Tibetan calendar and money and are Lamaism believing.

The name Moinba, formerly used as an epithet by the Tibetans, means "People Living in Moinyu". After the founding of new China, they were given the formal appellation the Moinba Nationality.

The Moinba language belongs to the Tibetan branch of the Tibeto-Burman group of the Sino-Tibetan family. As the language has no script, the Moinbas use the Tibetan language. The Tibetan New Year's Day is the most important festival of the Moinbas. In every July, they celebrate their "Fruit-Awaiting" Festival.

1
Crossing a rattan bridge.
2
A Moinba woman.
3
"Fruit-Awaiting" is a traditional festival among the Moinbas.
4
"May you have good scores in the archery competition."

THE LHOBAS

The Lhoba Nationality is one of the smallest ethnic groups of China. It has only 2,312 members. Now they mainly live in Mainling, Medog, Zayu, Lhunze and Nang counties.

The Lhobas have many tribes including the Bogar, Ningbo, Bangbo, Degen, Adi, and Tajin. Lhoba is a name given them by the Tibetans meaning "the Southerners". After the founding of new China, they were named the Lhoba Nationality.

The Lhoba language belongs to the Tibeto-Burman group of the Sino-Tibetan family with a distinct diversity of local dialects. In the past, the Lhobas summed and kept track of time by typing knots in rope and making notches on wood, but now some Lhobas use Tibetan to keep written records.

The west of the turn of the Yarlung Zangbo River in the southern Himalayan Range, is home of the Lhobas. This beautiful gorge area, covered with thick forests, is quite difficult for access. But the Lhobas managed to develop high skills in building plank road on cliff and passing rattan bridge, single-plank bridge and cable. By the mid-20th century, the Lhoba society was still at the rudimentary slash-and-burn stage in agriculture, which was supplemented by hunting. Ancient tradition remained. On group hunts, large games were equally shared in the tribe.

1
The Lhobas celebrate their *Xudulong* Festival with singing and dancing.
2
Lhoba men wear sabers around their waists.

3
Owing to lack of easy transport, Lhoba people have to carry their produce to places where they can exchange it for daily necessities.
4
A Lhoba women in her holiday array.

CHINA'S MINORITY PEOPLES

THE JINOS

The Jinos, with a population of 18,021, mainly live in the Jino Township of Jinghong County, Xishuangbanna Dai Autonomous Prefecture, Yunnan Province. A few can be found in Mengwang, Mengyang, Ganlanba and Dadugang of Jinghong County and Xiangming, Menglun of Mengla County.

The Jino Mountain Region where the Jinos make their homes has a tropical climate. The fertile land, with abundant rainfall and lush forests, produces a large amount of quality tea. The most famous is the Pu'er Tea. The Jinos took up farming in an ancient time. They plant rice, cotton and maize.

The word Jino, called "Youle" in Chinese in the past, refers to the descendants of a maternal uncle, because the Jino people show the greatest respect to their mother's brothers, who are traditionally worshipped by the family after their death. In June 1979, the Jino Nationality became the 55th ethnic group of China.

Various reasons deterred social progress among the Jinos. Until the 1950s, their society remained at the primitive commune stage. Slash-and-burn farming was prevalent. The Jino religion combines aboriginal animism with deep respect for ancestors.

The Jinos have no written form of their own and their spoken language belongs to the Tibeto-Burman Group of the Sino-Tibetan family. Formerly they kept records by making notches in bamboo.

1
A Jino woman playing a *kouxian* or mouth organ.
2
Beat a sun drum to celebrate the good harvest.
3
The Youle Mountain produces a large amount of bamboo. Musical instruments of bamboo can make beautiful melodies.
4
Blowing *xiao*, a vertical bamboo flute.
5
A bamboo arrow shooting competition among Jino children.

名誉主任:张家骅
编委主任:黄祖安
编　　委:施庆华 李春生 陈月萍 赵春林
主　　编: 李春生 陈 涌
翻　　译: 姜瀛
美术设计:史维平
封面题字:黄钟骏
本画册资料由中国画报社提供

编　　著:中国画报社
　　　　新世纪之光编辑委员会
出　　版:中国画报出版社
印　　制:北京东方明珠文化发展公司
地　　址:中国北京海淀上地四街八号
邮政编码:100085
电　　话:62983406—32
国外发行:中国国际图书贸易总公司
地　　址:中国北京海淀区车公庄西路35号
信　　箱:北京邮政信箱第399号
邮政编码:100044
开本 大16开 印张 6张
图片 306张 文字 50千
1995年8月第1版 1995年8月第1次印刷
1996年7月第2版 1996年7月第2次印刷

印数 3001—5000册
书号 ISBN7—80024—046—0/J－047
09600
85—E—469S

图书在版编目(CIP)数据

中国少数民族/中国画报出版社编 .－北京:中国画报出版社,1996.7重印
ISBN 7－80024－046－0

Ⅰ.中… Ⅱ.中…Ⅲ.少数民族－中国－摄影集 Ⅳ.K28－64
中国版本图书馆CIP数据核字(96)第11123号